# Caerwent Roman Town

Richard J. Brewer BA, FSA

# Roman Venta Silurum

## Revealing the Past

In 1586, the antiquary William Camden wrote of 'Venta, a very ancient city…, whose name neither the rage of men nor time has yet extinguished'. As seen today, Caerwent is a small village, but there is much to remind the visitor of its Roman past. In Roman times it was a town of considerable significance, the largest centre of civilian population in Wales. The town bore the name Venta Silurum — 'market of the Silures'. It was the administrative centre and capital of the Silures, whose territories included the latter-day counties of Brecknock, Glamorgan and Monmouthshire. Venta was sited on a slight rise in the middle of a broad open valley in an area of prime agricultural land, a little over 2 miles (3.2km) from the river Severn. It sat astride the main Roman coastal road running from Gloucester (Glevum) to Caerleon (Isca) and beyond.

Apart from being listed in the Antonine Itinerary — a third-century road book listing principal routes and stopping places — and the Ravenna Cosmography — a seventh-century topographical list based on much earlier information — Caerwent is not mentioned in Roman literature. Archaeologists have had, therefore, to dig up its remains to discover its history, what it looked like and how its inhabitants lived.

Numerous early topographical writers, from the fifteenth century onwards, described the appearance of Caerwent in their day and recorded various discoveries. The first to leave an account of any substance was John Leland (writing about 1540), who described Caerwent as 'sumtyme a fair and a large cyte'. But by this time the ruins of any internal buildings had all but vanished — robbed to build new cottages.

During the late eighteenth and early nineteenth centuries, Caerwent lay on the well-trodden route of tourists in search of the historical and picturesque

in Wales. Among others, H. P. Wyndham, William Coxe, G. W. Manby, and Edward Donovan all recorded their impressions. Samuel Seyer, the Bristol historian, left a description of the grubbing-up of Roman walls for their limestone and its burning into lime, a fact all too clearly borne out by archaeological excavation. The interest of local people, however, was not aroused; there were no 'crop marks' from buried walling, and the few random discoveries led only to a pecuniary interest on the part of the villagers.

Both Manby (1802) and Donovan (1805) tell of the fate of a rich pavement found in 1777. At first, as Manby recorded, it had been preserved with vigilance by the landowner, who had erected a building over it. The landowner's concern for the pavement was not to last, however, for when he chose to build a brewhouse he 'uncovered the edifice in order to save expense, and thus exposed it to vandalism and weather'. During his visit, Manby had

*Opposite: The hooded bust of winter, holding a billhook, from the 'Seasons' mosaic discovered in 1901 during the archaeological investigation of House XI.7S in Caerwent. Although the remains of the Roman town of Venta Silurum were often mentioned by the tourists who visited Caerwent in the late eighteenth and early nineteenth centuries, no significant archaeological exploration took place there before 1855. House XI.7S was uncovered during the series of excavations conducted between 1899 and 1913 that established the ground plan of Venta (Newport Museum and Art Gallery).*

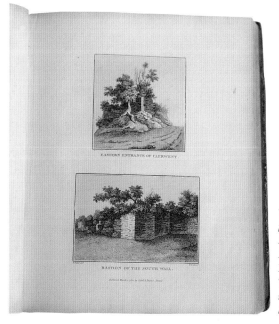

EASTERN ENTRANCE OF CAERWENT

BASTION OF THE SOUTH WALL.

*Two vignettes of the Roman features at Caerwent in Archdeacon William Coxe's* An Historical Tour in Monmouthshire *(London 1801). The upper drawing shows the remains of the east gate and the lower a tower on the south wall.*

*Above: Octavius Morgan (1803–88), a notable antiquary and Member of Parliament for Monmouthshire for thirty-four years, undertook the first significant archaeological work at Caerwent when he revealed a bath house and another building in the south-east corner of the town (Private collection).*

*Above right: Godfrey Morgan (1831–1913), second Baron and first Viscount Tredegar, was elected president of the newly created 'Caerwent Exploration Fund' in September 1899. He provided generous financial support for the Fund's excavations at Caerwent until they drew to a close in 1913 (Tredegar House, Newport).*

to drive a sow and her piglets from the spot, where they had been rooting. Donovan later tried to save the remaining piece of scrollwork decoration by having a window shutter laid over it.

In 1855, the first archaeological excavations of any significance were initiated by Octavius Morgan (1803–88), a notable antiquary and for many years Member of Parliament for Monmouthshire. Limited investigations in the south-east corner of the town (*Insula* XX), at the site of the mosaic unearthed in 1777, revealed part of a small bath house together with another building. But this work was not followed up for many years.

The known ground plan of *Venta* (inside back cover) is largely the result of excavations which took place between 1899 and 1913. The work was instigated by the Clifton Antiquarian Club of Bristol, founded in 1884 to arrange meetings and excursions for the study of objects of archaeological interest in the west of England and south Wales. In 1899, after conducting successful trial explorations in the south-west corner of the town, the club agreed a scheme of work. A committee was formed (to be known as the 'Caerwent Exploration Fund') and Lord Tredegar (1831–1913), a local benefactor, was elected as president. The excavations were to be funded by

*Right: Excavators at Caerwent, about 1900. Thomas Ashby, one of the two men mainly responsible for the supervision of the early excavations, appears on the right wearing a Norfolk jacket.*

public subscription, but the response was generally poor, and the works had to be financed more and more from Lord Tredegar's own pocket.

The supervision of the excavations fell mainly to two members of the club: Alfred Hudd, a man of independent means and an excellent local antiquary, and Thomas Ashby (who was to become director of the British School at Rome). At that time, the recovery of the plan, the structural features and the function of each building investigated were the chief attainable ends, for archaeological techniques were still in their infancy. The normal procedure was to drive diagonal trenches across the site; any structure found was isolated and cleared to floor-level. In most cases, the excavators were content to explore only the uppermost Roman buildings, leaving untouched any earlier structures, especially those built of timber and clay, which they could scarcely recognize. By the time the excavations drew to a close in 1913, almost two-thirds of the town had been explored in a vast number of trenches. The resulting plan, however, was essentially that of the late Roman town, and very little light was thrown on the origins and early development of *Venta*. Many of the finds from these excavations are displayed in Newport Museum and Art Gallery. The collection was given to Newport by the third Baron Tredegar in 1916.

The periodic investigations carried out since the conclusion of these large-scale explorations have generally been of a more limited nature. Within the town, part of the public baths was uncovered in 1923 and, during 1946 and 1947, excavations in an area next to Pound Lane (pp. 46–51) revealed the foundations of shops and a large courtyard house (VII.26N and 27N) which were subsequently laid out for public display. The defences have also received attention over the years and there have been several investigations. The most extensive was carried out in 1925 on the south side of the town by V. E. Nash-Williams (1897–1955) of the National Museum of Wales. In 1973, excavations beyond the defences, just outside the east gate, were concerned with a substantial early medieval cemetery.

All this was done as opportunity offered. Fortunately, since the 1930s, judicious application of the Ancient Monuments and Town and Country Planning Acts has prevented any development in the conservation area, apart from very modest extensions, within the Roman defences. Hence, Caerwent presents one of the very few opportunities not only to investigate large areas of a Roman town, but also to

display the remains of the excavated buildings to the public. In 1981, a new series of research excavations was initiated by the National Museum of Wales, a programme conducted jointly with Cadw, the historic environment service of the Welsh Assembly Government, from 1984 to 1995. The work has added immeasurably to our knowledge of *Venta*, especially of its origins and early development.

Three sites were investigated between 1981 and 1995: a large courtyard house in the north-west corner of the town (I.28N); the *forum-basilica* (VIII) at the very heart of the town; and the adjacent Romano-Celtic temple (IX). These buildings have now been consolidated and interpreted for public presentation.

*Above: A late first-century face-pot, found near the Roman public bath building at Caerwent in 1923 (National Museum of Wales).*

*Left: V. E. Nash-Williams (1897–1955) of the National Museum of Wales, shown here at the Roman fortress at Caerleon, supervised the excavation of the public baths in 1923 and the investigation of the southern defences in 1925 (National Museum of Wales).*

*Below: Entrance hall of the Romano-Celtic temple. One of the recently excavated sites at Caerwent, 1981–91 (National Museum of Wales).*

*Right: When the Romans pushed into south-east Wales in the second half of the first century AD, the region was occupied by the Silures. They put up a determined resistance to the Roman advance and the historian, Tacitus, described them as powerful, warlike, valiant and stubborn. This artist's impression shows a Silurian warrior (Illustration by Geraint Derbyshire).*

*Above: A bronze harness mount inlaid with enamel found in Silurian territory near Chepstow. It dates to the end of the Iron Age (National Museum of Wales).*

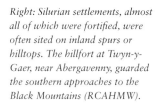

*Right: Silurian settlements, almost all of which were fortified, were often sited on inland spurs or hilltops. The hillfort at Twyn-y-Gaer, near Abergavenny, guarded the southern approaches to the Black Mountains (RCAHMW).*

# The Silures and the Roman Occupation of Wales

At the time of the Roman conquest, south-east Wales was inhabited by a tribe known as the Silures. The Roman historian Tacitus describes the tribe in words which, few as they are, conjure up a vivid glimpse of their appearance:

'... the swarthy faces of the Silures and the prevalence of curly hair among them combine with the fact that Spain lies opposite to confirm that the ancient Iberians crossed over and took possession of those parts'.

It is most unlikely that the Silures had their origin in Spain, and Tacitus's remark was based on a doubtless reasonable comparison of the physical traits of the two peoples, and also on his mistaken notion of the geographical relationship and nearness of Britain and Spain. More to the point, Tacitus also describes the Silures as powerful, warlike, valiant and stubborn.

The Silures appear to have lived predominantly on or near the better soils of the coastal zone, although most of their territory lay in the densely wooded uplands, which were to prove ideal for guerilla warfare. Their settlements, almost all of them fortified, were very often on coastal promontories as at Sudbrook, or on inland spurs as at Llanmelin (pp. 54–56), or on the tops of hills such as Lodge Hill Camp, near Caerleon, and Twyn-y-Gaer, near

Abergavenny. They varied in size from small farmsteads to large sites of many acres housing a number of families. The Gwent Levels, although subject to extensive flooding, have also provided evidence of settlements. In the Iron Age a system of brushwood trackways allowed wet areas to be crossed. At Goldcliff Point seven rectangular Iron Age timber buildings have been excavated, and the surfaces surrounding them retained large numbers of cattle hoof prints as well as human footprints. Overlooking the Levels, a small enclosed settlement at Thornwell Farm, near Chepstow, was occupied from the Late Bronze Age through to the Roman period. Nearly all the population would have depended on farming for their livelihood.

For some time it was thought that the hillfort at Llanmelin served as the pre-Roman tribal capital of the Silures. The main reason for this suggestion is its proximity to Caerwent, just over a mile (1.6km) to the south-east; but Llanmelin appears to be no different from the many other small and medium-sized Silurian forts. In fact, there is no obvious claimant for the status of regional capital. It would appear, from the lack of any tribal centre, that clan and family ties were perhaps more important than tribal ones. It was only when their independence was threatened that the Silures were able to unite and fight under a single banner, and then it was to be under the command of a great war leader from another tribe.

After their initial invasion in AD 43, the Roman forces swept quickly across the southern part of Britain. However, their advance soon faltered when they came up against the harsher landscape of Wales and the more resilient opposition of its tribes. Raids into the new province, partly instigated by Caratacus, the defeated British leader who had sought refuge among the Silures, opened a chapter of some thirty years' campaigning in the west of Britain. The fighting was often bitter, even after Caratacus had been defeated and handed over to the Romans in AD 51. In the following year the Roman army was to suffer its greatest defeat in Britain, when it lost a large part of a legion in a battle with the Silures.

Despite this setback, the Romans were soon to gain the upper hand, moving against the Silures on a wide front. By the mid-50s, with the establishment of a fortress at Usk, they had brought the southern coastal belt and the area to the east of the river Usk

under Roman control. By AD 60 the Roman army was close to victory, after the governor Suetonius Paulinus had carried out successful campaigns against the tribes in both south and north Wales. But a devastating revolt led by Boudicca, queen of the Iceni in Norfolk, brought the conquest to a temporary halt. The work required in restoring the ravaged province prevented further campaigns in Wales for over a decade.

It was not until the arrival of a new governor, Julius Frontinus, in AD 74, that attention was once again turned towards the reduction of Wales. The Second Augustan Legion moved to a new legionary fortress built at Caerleon (Isca). From this base the Silures were subdued, and a network of forts was established to prevent any further gathering of hostile forces.

*A silver coin of Caratacus, the leader of British resistance to Rome, who sought refuge among the Silures. He was eventually defeated and handed over to the Romans in AD 51 (National Museum of Wales).*

*Julius Frontinus, governor of Britain from AD 74 to 77, was appointed to complete the conquest of the Welsh tribes. In 74 or 75, he led the Second Augustan Legion to their new fortress at Caerleon and defeated the fierce Silures. This artist's impression depicts a legionary soldier of Legio II Augusta (Illustration by Geraint Derbyshire).*

*Comfortable romanized farms developed in the prime agricultural areas of south Wales. This illustration shows the Roman villa at Llantwit Major in the Vale of Glamorgan as it may have appeared in the early fourth century (National Museum of Wales).*

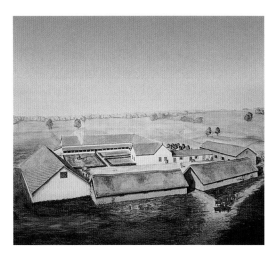

The Roman army was not merely an instrument of conquest, but it was also the means whereby a number of Roman institutions and practices were introduced to the native inhabitants. These included the enforcement of peace and law, the use of coinage, and the Latin language for official purposes and as a desirable social attainment. Architects and surveyors within the army introduced various techniques in building and water engineering.

In due course, the Silures of the coastal belt, whatever the reaction of the hill-folk, gradually adopted romanized ways under the shadow of the Second Augustan Legion at Caerleon, and were eventually granted a form of local government with a capital at Caerwent. Other civilian settlements grew up outside the legionary fortress at Caerleon and at some of its auxiliary forts, where the troops provided a profitable market for traders. Several roadside settlements were to develop on former military sites at Usk, Monmouth, Abergavenny and Chepstow. At Cowbridge, on the road between Caerwent and Carmarthen, a 'small town' developed, probably as a market centre for surrounding farms in the Vale of Glamorgan.

In the countryside there was a diversity of settlement types, ranging from substantial villas — best considered as romanized farmsteads — to those of humble character, which display few Roman trappings or influence. The known rural settlement pattern is largely restricted to the lowlands of the Vale of Glamorgan and Monmouthshire occupying the best quality land. Both cereal cultivation and pastoral farming were important components of the economy. The Gwent Levels, which provided excellent grazing for cattle, sheep and horses, were also utilized and considerable resources were expended to drain these damp pasturelands.

Further to the west were the Demetae, the only other tribe in Wales which was possibly granted self-government. It is widely held that the Roman town at Carmarthen (*Moridunum*) served as their tribal capital. Throughout the rest of Wales, under more or less constant military surveillance, there were no further towns; though Kenchester on the Wye, Wroxeter on the Severn, and Whitchurch, further north, lay close to an otherwise largely military zone. There were also civil settlements outside some of the auxiliary forts.

## Roman Wales

N

*Segontium*
(Caernarfon)

DECEANGLI

ORDOVICES

DEMETAE

SILURES

Chester

Whitchurch

Wroxeter

Kenchester

Brecon

Carmarthen

Loughor

Neath

Cowbridge

Llantwit Major

Caerleon

Caerwent

Cardiff

Sea Mills

### Military Sites

Legionary ▣

Auxiliary ■

Fortlet ▪

### Civil Sites

Capital ◉

Other ●

Romanized Farm ▲

### Mines

Copper Ⓒ    Gold Ⓖ

Iron Ⓘ    Lead Ⓛ

Roads ----

| 0 | 15 | 30 Kilometres |

| 0 | 10 | 20 Miles |

# The Foundation and Status of Venta Silurum

Evidence from coins, pottery, glass and metalwork points to the foundation of a settlement at Caerwent only a few years after the Roman conquest of south Wales had been achieved by the legionary forces. The manufacture of pottery by civilians for the military market, although probably short lived, appears to have been an important activity in the development of early *Venta Silurum*. However, little is known about the character of the early settlement, though it is unlikely that there were any defences, and most of the internal buildings were doubtless of timber construction.

The growth of a settlement at Caerwent, so soon after the conquest, is perhaps not surprising. We should bear in mind that it was located in an area of Silurian territory which had been under Roman control since the mid-50s, some twenty years before the rest of south Wales. *Venta* was also in easy reach of the Welsh terminal of the Severn ferry, which was established in Roman times between Sudbrook and Sea Mills (*Abona*) on the Bristol Avon. From the muddy foreshore at Black Rock, Portskewett, just to

*Under the shadow of the Second Augustan Legion at Caerleon, the Silures gradually adopted romanized ways. Their capital was located in Caerwent,* Venta Silurum, *seen in this aerial view from the west. The road running through the centre of the present village follows the line of the main Roman road. The walls enclose an area of some 44 acres (18ha), making* Venta *one of the smallest tribal capitals of Roman Britain (RCAHMW).*

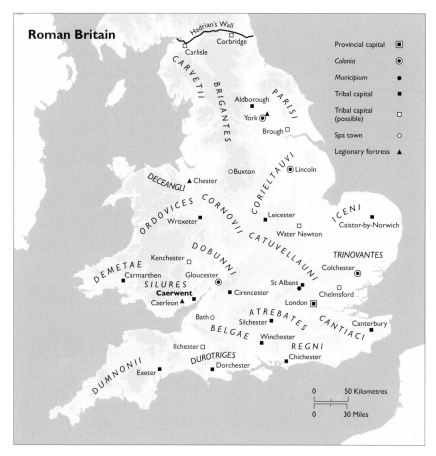

*Top right: A selection of the many coins discovered on the foreshore at Black Rock, Portskewett. This group ranges from a coin of Nero, struck AD 62–68, to one of the house of Valentinian, struck AD 364–78 (Newport Museum and Art Gallery).*

*Above right: The* colonia *at Lincoln — one of four such colonies of veterans established in Roman Britain — was founded in the first century. A large portion of the third-century north gate still survives (City of Lincoln Council).*

the north of Sudbrook, a large number of Roman coins has been retrieved. These coins span some 300 years of Roman occupation, ranging from the Emperor Claudius (AD 41–54) to the house of Theodosius (AD 388–402). It may not be too fanciful to think of them as offerings to a river god, made by travellers on the ferry in return for a safe crossing.

Following their surrender, the Silures would have become *dediticii* — a people without any political status or rights — to be dealt with as the Romans pleased. However, the Roman administration had good reason for showing moderation. The cost of maintaining a large garrison was enormous. There were also difficulties in supplying the army in some of the more remote forts, and, furthermore, manpower was limited. The whole history of the military occupation of Wales is one, therefore, of reduction in the garrisons wherever possible — either by abandoning forts completely or, if this were not possible, by introducing smaller units in place of larger ones. The more successful the attempt to

mollify and civilize the native population, the more rapidly this process could begin and continue.

It is against this background that we may see the creation of the *Civitas Silurum*, whereby political identity was returned to the tribe. The Silures were granted, under close Roman supervision, a form of self-government with their own council. This process had already been carried out in the rest of southern Britain where there had been peace for several decades. By granting self-government to many of the British tribes, the Romans managed to shift much of the burden of local administration — legal duties, tax collecting and public works — on to the shoulders of the natives.

In Britain, as elsewhere in the empire, there were various kinds of self-governing communities. Foremost were the *coloniae*, communities of Roman citizens, intended for veteran legionaries. Colchester, Lincoln and Gloucester were founded as such in the first century. A fourth, at York, was perhaps not established until the end of the second or early third century. Ranking below the colony was another type of chartered community, the *municipium*, of which St Albans (*Verulamium*) was an early and the only known British example. The constitutions of the *coloniae* and *municipia*, which controlled a fairly wide area (*territorium*), were on the model of Rome itself, with an elected council and magistrates.

The other recognized communities were of native peoples, or — as the Romans called them — 'foreign' (*civitates peregrinae*). For the most part they were formed from the existing pre-Roman tribal divisions. They had romanized administrations, possibly modelled on those of the chartered communities,

*The only known British example of a municipium was St Albans (Verulamium). The view shows the remains of the Roman theatre (© St Albans Museums).*

# The Paulinus Inscription

The existence of a *Civitas Silurum* is recorded on a fine statue base found at Caerwent in 1903. It had been reused as part of a post-Roman construction of heavy blocks in the centre of the village; the war memorial now stands on it. The stone can be seen today in the porch of St Stephen's church.

The inscription is dedicated to Tiberius Claudius Paulinus, who had been commander of the Second Augustan Legion at Caerleon, a post he held during the reign of the Emperor Caracalla (AD 211–17). After leaving Caerleon, Paulinus held office in two Gallic provinces, *Gallia Narbonensis* and *Gallia Lugdunensis*. Paulinus evidently performed some helpful act or made some gift to the Silures, and in return they honoured him with the erection of a statue and a record of his career. In AD 220, he returned as governor of *Britannia Inferior*, the more northerly of the two provinces into which the island had been divided by the Emperor Septimius Severus (AD 198–211) at the beginning of the third century. The Caerwent stone does not record Paulinus's governorship of *Britannia Inferior*, and it may be presumed, therefore, that it was set up a short time before he took up the post.

The Caerwent inscription is one of the most important to have been found in Roman Britain; besides giving details of the typical mixed military and civilian career of a Roman governor, it also throws light on the local civil administration.

*Above: This third-century coin issued from Alexandria in the Troad (modern Turkey) depicts the city council in session. The Silures were granted self-government with their own council probably in the early second century (National Museum of Wales).*

*Left: The Paulinus inscription is carved on a statue base now situated in the church porch at Caerwent. The inscription was originally of twelve lines, but the first line of Latin text has now been lost. It reads: '[To Tiberius Claudius] Paulinus, (once) commander of the Second Augustan Legion, (next) proconsul of the province of Gallia Narbonensis, (now) imperial governor of the province of Lugdunensis; by decree of the council of the community of the state of the Silures.'*

It tells us that the tribe was administered by a council, or *ordo*, that could pass decrees. Since the erection of the inscription was an act of the tribal council on behalf of the whole of the Silures, rather than just the town of *Venta Silurum*, it clearly demonstrates that a *civitas* should be seen, as it were, as an area of territory with a town in the middle, rather than as a town with territory round it as a Roman *colonia* would have been.

but the inhabitants merely possessed their tribal, rather than Roman, citizenship. As time went on, however, Roman citizenship was increasingly acquired on an individual basis. Then, in AD 212, the Roman franchise was extended to provincials generally under the terms of the famous edict of Caracalla (AD 211–17), known as the *Constitutio Antoniniana*.

Each established native *civitas* needed a centre where the tribal council could meet, law courts could be set up, and other administrative duties carried out. The coupling of the tribal name with the place name allows us to identify a number of the principal administrative centres in Roman Britain, as in the case of *Venta Silurum* itself.

Exactly when the Silures were granted self-government we do not know. However, it is generally held that the presence of a *forum-basilica* complex in a town — the seat of local government — is sufficient indication of the existence of such a native community. Excavations on the site of the *forum-basilica* at Caerwent indicate that the building was first erected in the earlier part of the second century AD, probably at the time of the Emperor Hadrian (AD 117–38). It would appear, therefore, that the

Silures had passed from military control and had been granted self-government by this date if not before, and that *Venta* had been chosen as their tribal capital. This situation is also reflected in the withdrawal of garrisons from south-east Wales for service on Hadrian's Wall.

The creation of a *civitas* in a newly conquered area is described by the Roman historian, Tacitus, and concerns the Frisii, a tribe to the north of the Rhine. Tacitus tells us that after a rebellion, in AD 47, the tribe gave the Roman general, Corbulo, hostages and that he marked out their territory and imposed a council, magistrates and a legal system. A similar process was probably followed by the governor of Britain in the setting up of the *Civitas Silurum*. Precise arrangements were necessary, particularly in marking out the lands allocated to the tribe. Boundaries had to be determined, not only with other tribes but also with the territory retained by the army for grazing its cattle and horses, as well as for farming. We can only guess where these boundaries ran; though to the east it was probably the Wye that marked the division with the Dobunni. It has been claimed that an inscription from the coast at Goldcliff, which

*Right: Caerwent's forum-basilica complex, the seat of local government, was probably erected at the time of the Emperor Hadrian (AD 117–38). This bronze head of Hadrian was found in the river Thames in 1834 (©The Trustees of the British Museum).*

*Far right: This inscribed stone was found at Goldcliff in 1878 and reads: 'The century of Stratorius Maximus of the first cohort constructed 33 1/2 paces.' The stone may have acted as a marker between legionary pastures and the land allocated to the self-governing Silures (National Museum of Wales).*

records the construction of a length of sea bank or drainage dyke by legionary labour, is related to a boundary between Silurian and military grazing land south-west of Caerwent. There is also some evidence for legionary involvement in land reclamation on the tidal salt marshes of the Wentlooge Levels between the Usk and Rhymney rivers, particularly when considering the scale of the drainage works.

Written sources provide details of the rites that the Romans performed when founding a new city and marking its boundaries. The Romans believed that these rituals had been handed down from the Etruscans and that Romulus had followed the same practices when he founded Rome in 753 BC. The first religious rite involved seeking divine intervention in the choice of location for the city. A veiled diviner (*augur*) would then fix the boundaries using a wand, before a sacred furrow was ploughed around the limits of the city. Although there is no certain evidence for such ceremonies in the foundation of towns in Britain, these ritual practices are known to have taken place in other parts of the Roman empire. The importance of these rituals lay in defining and blessing the urban space; in other words they spiritually and physically marked the boundary between town and country. When the boundaries of the town had been set, the surveyor would lay out the town using the customary Roman proportions. It has been suggested that the earth-and-timber defences and masonry walls enclosing the tribal capitals may preserve the original boundaries in monumental form.

*Below: Goldcliff Point on the Severn estuary seen from the air. Large areas of the Gwent Levels were first drained and the land reclaimed during the Roman period. These wetlands would have provided excellent grazing for both horses and cattle (RCAHMW).*

*Left: This small Roman statuette, found near Piercebridge in County Durham, depicts a plough drawn by a bull and a cow. This unusual pairing suggests that this is not an ordinary agricultural scene, but rather a representation of the ceremony of ritual ploughing around a newly founded city. The use of a bull and cow on such occasions was considered to bring good luck and fertility. Such a ceremony may have been performed at the foundation of Venta Silurum (© The Trustees of the British Museum).*

*Above: This painting of Roman Caerwent by Alan Sorrell (1904–74) shows the town divided by streets into a total of twenty rectangular plots known as* insulae. *A great deal of research has been undertaken on Roman towns since this painting was completed in 1937, and ideas and interpretations have changed. Nevertheless, Sorrell's work still conveys well enough an impression of Caerwent as it may have appeared in the fourth century (National Museum of Wales).*

*Above right: The population of most Romano-British towns would have been a mix of both native inhabitants and a smaller migrant element, mainly traders and veteran soldiers. This fine tombstone from York shows a typical family group. It was set up for Flavia Augustina by her husband, a veteran of the Sixth Legion (York Museums Trust / Yorkshire Museum).*

# Inside the Roman Town

The town walls form a quadrilateral of some 44 acres (18ha), making *Venta Silurum* one of the smallest tribal capitals of Roman Britain. Irregularities in the outline shape of the town walls — each side is slightly convex and all the corners are blunted — no doubt reflect, in part, the natural lie of the ground.

In common with other tribal capitals, *Venta* eventually had a planned system of streets dividing the town into rectangular plots (*insulae*), here numbering twenty, which contained the public buildings, shops, houses and farms. Each *insula*, although not uniformly laid out, was probably intended to be 275 Roman feet square (one *pes* = 11 3/4 inches; 0.296m) in the planned scheme. The council would have been responsible for the laying and upkeep of the roads in and around Caerwent. The roads were surfaced with rammed gravel, and had cambered sides so that rainwater could run off. Roads of this type needed regular resurfacing, so that in places a great thickness of road material built up.

The most recent excavations have cast doubt on the extent of the early settlement. It would appear that in the late first century AD, and for much of the second, *Venta* was no more than a sprawl along the main Roman road to Caerleon. The regular layout of the full street grid does not seem to have been established in its final form much before the beginning of the third century. The wealth of *Venta* in comparison with some other towns is striking, inviting the thought that it attracted comparatively wealthy veterans of the Second Augustan Legion to settle there.

The population of a Romano-British town is hard to estimate. Even at Caerwent, where the town plan is relatively complete, it is uncertain how many buildings were occupied at any one time and how many people lived in each house. Comparative studies of urban population densities (ranging from 55–87 people per acre; 137–216 per ha), considered to be typical in the pre-industrial era, would suggest a figure of anywhere between 2,400 and 3,800 inhabitants for *Venta* in the third and fourth centuries. This estimate, however, may be somewhat high, for the density of building at Caerwent is apparently low.

## Public Buildings

At the centre of the town's public life was the *forum-basilica* (marketplace and civic hall), which appropriately occupied the whole of the central building block (*Insula* VIII), north of the main Roman street. This is where the council (*ordo*) of the tribe would meet, and local justice would be administered. The *forum-basilica* dominated the townscape and would have been seen as an important symbol of civic pride and a statement of *romanitas*. Part of this grand building has been excavated and is on view to the public (pp. 38–43).

Towns also contained sacred places, since the affairs of government needed divine guidance, and communities were bound together by festivals organized in honour of the civic and other deities. The sites of several temples are known at *Venta Silurum*: one to the east of the *forum* (*Insula* IX), which has been excavated and remains on display (pp. 45–46); another to the south of the main street (*Insula* XII), while a third may have been sited outside the east gate (pp. 36–37). A shrine,

no doubt dedicated to the emperor and the civic deities, was also incorporated in the rear range of rooms of the *basilica*.

In the Roman world the public bath house was a very important feature of the town. It not only provided somewhere to wash, but also a place where the citizens could take exercise, play games, gossip or just relax. At Caerwent some of the larger houses had their own private bath suites, but most people would have visited the public baths that were built on the opposite side of the main street from the *forum* (*Insula* XIII). The baths were excavated in 1923, but unfortunately, because of modern farm buildings, it was only possible to uncover the northern half.

Another public building was the *mansio*, a form of inn or stopping place, where officials and couriers of the imperial posting service (*cursus publicus*) would lodge and change horses. At Caerwent, the large building that lay immediately on the left of those entering through the south gate has been interpreted as a *mansio* (XVIII.12S). The building was arranged round three sides of a

*Above: Towns like Caerwent contained various sacred places, including public temples and domestic shrines. This statuette of a mother goddess was found in a pit near the Romano-Celtic temple (pp. 45–46) in 1908 (Newport Museum and Art Gallery).*

*Below: An imaginative reconstruction of the second-century forum-basilica at Wroxeter, Shropshire; although similar in form, it was much larger than the complex at Caerwent (Illustration by Ivan Lapper: English Heritage).*

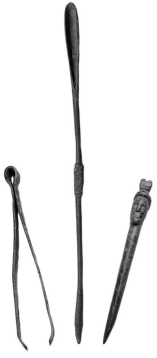

*Above: That the residents of Caerwent were concerned with their appearance and personal hygiene is reflected by the many toiletry items, like those shown above, found in the town (Newport Museum and Art Gallery).*

*Above right: The excavation of a Roman well in Caerwent around 1900. Although an aqueduct provided water from the hills to the north for the public baths, the* basilica *and some of the larger houses, most of the residents of* Venta Silurum *would have depended upon wells for water (National Museum of Wales).*

*Opposite: Scenes popular in Roman funerary art on the Continent enable us to repeople Caerwent's shops with their busy artisans. In this relief a Roman cutler displays the neatly racked stock on his stall to a customer. Numerous iron knives and tools have been discovered in the town at Caerwent (© Photo SCALA, Florence — Galleria Lapidaria, Vatican, Vatican City).*

courtyard, with the fourth side being enclosed by a wall built against the town rampart. A large forecourt stretched across the front of the building, where travellers would have dismounted from their horses. Of the numerous rooms, several were equipped with hypocausts, and a fine mosaic was discovered in the large room in the north-west corner. A sizeable latrine, with a sewer on three sides, above which would have been wooden seating, lay in the corner of the courtyard, and seems to indicate a building of more than merely domestic character.

The presence of wooden water pipes running southwards from the north gate and a large drain flowing under the south gate show that fresh water was brought to the town by an aqueduct from the hills to the north. Most of the water would have been channelled to the public baths, the *basilica*, and a few of the larger houses. The waste water was used to flush out latrines and the other main drains. For domestic purposes, most residents would have drawn water from wells.

### Trade and Occupations

The prosperity of a town was largely dependent on the wealth, mainly derived from agriculture and other natural resources, of the area it served. Important, too, were the drive and enthusiasm of the inhabitants and the type and diversity of the goods and services that they provided.

One of the main functions of *Venta Silurum*, as its name indicates, was to act as a market centre for the surrounding countryside. Trade was given official encouragement with the provision of the *forum*, where shops could be rented and temporary stalls set up on market days. The buildings that crowded the main street frontages, except for the public edifices and one or two houses, were occupied by shopkeepers and craftsmen. These took the form of narrow strip buildings, which were aligned so as to present a gable-end to the street. At the front was the shop itself with a wide entrance, which could be closed by wooden shutters; a covered portico was often added to protect the goods on display and provide shelter for customers. The workshops were set behind, and at the rear, or possibly above, were the family's living quarters.

The shops might be owned by their inhabitants, or run by tenant freedmen or slave managers. Most of the shops occupied single plots, separated by narrow passages. These passages were designed not so much for access to the rear as for gutters catching rainwater from the roofs. Some of the shops were, however, 'semi-detached', of which XIII.27S is a good example. In one instance (under the later house XI.15S), there were two blocks of double shops, which were set closely together and shared a common portico. This arrangement would seem to imply that the block was under single ownership, and let as individual premises to tenants. With the shops so close to each other, expansion could only take place either by extending to the rear, or, as frequently occurred, by encroaching on the street. Some shopkeepers became prosperous enough to take over neighbouring premises, which generally enabled them to improve their living quarters. In one case, the owner of shop VII.26N was wealthy enough by the mid-fourth century to lay mosaics in two of the rooms.

There is little indication of the trades carried out on individual premises because the goods on sale would have been sold off or removed before closing down. Nevertheless, we might expect food shops selling produce brought in from the surrounding countryside, as well as oil and wine imported in amphorae and barrels from Spain and Gaul. Other shops would have stocked pottery and glass vessels, tools and cloth. It is not known to what extent bakers' shops existed, since grain was home ground

# A Selection of Roman Pottery from Caerwent

Everyday pottery, together with high-quality tableware, survives in vast quantities from Caerwent. Some pottery was made locally, but supplies also came, for example, from Dorset and Oxfordshire, and from elsewhere in Britain. More exotic wares were imported from overseas, often from very great distances. Many of the samples shown here can now be seen in Newport Museum and Art Gallery.

▼ A bowl of 'black-burnished' ware, from Dorset (National Museum of Wales).

② A handled jar in a grey fabric, made locally at the Caldicot kilns.

③ These two vessels, a colour-coated bowl and a pedestal vase, are products of the Oxfordshire kilns.

4a 4b Two examples of the best Roman tableware, known as samian. It was imported in vast quantities from south (4a) and central Gaul (4b), France, in the first and second centuries.

⑤ A small beaker of Rhenish colour-coated ware from the Rhine–Moselle area.

⑥ The neck of a large amphora, in which olive oil was transported from southern Spain. The handle is stamped with the initials used by the exporter: P.S.

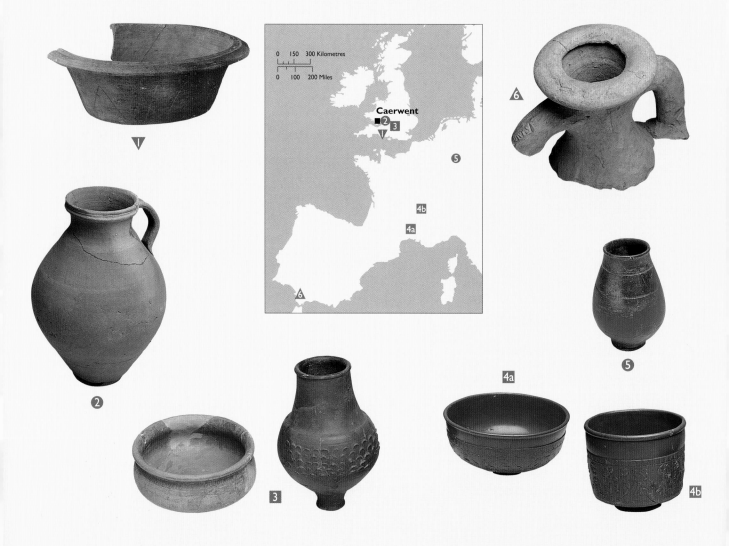

and also probably home baked. Likewise, the spinning of wool appears to have remained a domestic occupation, to judge from the number of spindle whorls found in private houses.

Some workshops were equipped with furnaces used in petty manufacturing operations, generally by metalworkers. Blacksmiths and bronzesmiths were required to supply tools to farmers and other craftsmen, as well as household goods such as locks and keys, bronze vessels and ornaments. Lead was also widely used by plumbers for piping, as sheeting for the manufacture of tanks, and for various small items such as weights. Other trades can be inferred from the many tools found, such as those belonging to carpenters, builders and decorators, while a shoe last may have come from a cobbler's shop. Many of the craftsmen's tools resemble those of the present day.

Pottery survives in vast quantities from Caerwent. The best tableware, samian, was imported from Gaul during the first and second centuries AD, and is a common find on town sites. Everyday coarse pottery, however, used in the kitchen for storage and the preparation of food, was manufactured at numerous local centres throughout Britain. Amongst those supplying *Venta* were the 'black-burnished' potteries of Dorset and the Oxfordshire kilns. Some pottery was also produced locally; an excavation at Caldicot, to the south-east of the town, revealed six kilns and hundreds of spoilt pots that had been discarded. The Caldicot potters were active in the third century, and produced a variety of bowls and jars in a grey fabric.

Besides the tradesmen, *Venta* would also have attracted skilled professional people such as doctors, teachers, architects and surveyors.

The legionary soldiers at Caerleon were close enough to Caerwent for them to have been an important source of income for the shopkeepers of the town. No doubt many of the legionaries would have travelled the short distance from *Isca* to *Venta*, to spend some of their leisure time in the shops and inns.

Some of the inhabitants of *Venta* would have been directly employed in agriculture, with corn, wool, beef and hides probably the most important produce. Numerous agricultural implements have been found in the town; some of these would have been for sale to outlying farms, but others could have been used

*Above: The remains of forges in a number of workshops point to the activity of metalworkers, who would have supplied the inhabitants of* Venta Silurum *with tools and household goods. This second-century AD relief shows a coppersmith at work (Museo Nazionale Atestino, Este/ Bridgeman Art Library).*

*Left: Three iron agricultural implements found in the town: a billhook, a mattock or hoe, and a pair of shears (Newport Museum and Art Gallery).*

on farms that existed within the town. Some houses were surrounded by yards and paddocks in which there were cottages for farm workers and agricultural buildings, such as barns and byres. These farms lay on the fringes of the town, for example II.1N and II.2N were situated near the north gate, and another, XI.7S, was close to the west gate. Farmers would have grazed their cattle and sheep and grown crops on the land within and immediately surrounding the town. A large elliptical enclosure in the north-east corner of the town (*Insula* IV) — constructed at a late stage in the town's history, for it overlay the foundations of several demolished buildings — was originally identified as an amphitheatre, but is now thought more likely to have served as a livestock market.

*Above: Part of a roof finial in the form of a pine cone from building XII.20S. Elsewhere in Caerwent, the gable-end of buildings with stone roofs often carried a finial in the form of a lantern (Newport Museum and Art Gallery).*

*Above right: A diagrammatic reconstruction of House XVI.3S. The central courtyard probably served as a garden and contained a statue base. Most of the rooms were entered directly from the surrounding portico.*

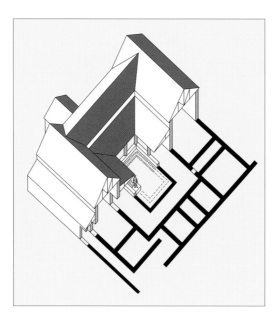

### Private Houses

Several different types of house have been excavated at Caerwent, ranging from modest dwellings to very large houses that provided luxurious living accommodation. As we have seen, most of the craftsmen and traders lived behind, or possibly above, their shops. The larger houses would have been occupied by wealthier merchants, members of the council and possibly veterans from the legion at Caerleon.

The simplest houses consisted of rectangular blocks, divided into rooms, entered from corridors that ran along one, or more often both sides. The corridors maintained the privacy of the rooms which otherwise could be reached only from one another. More elaborate houses had two or more blocks situated around an enclosed courtyard, which may have been laid out as a garden. These houses were usually of a sprawling design, because land — except in the very centre of the town — was abundant. Several houses were of a more compact design being arranged round all four sides of a colonnaded courtyard, as was the Mediterranean fashion. These houses were inward facing with the intention, in Italy, of providing quiet from the bustle of the busy streets and shade from the hot sun. Most typical of this design is House XVI.3S in the south-west corner of the town. The remains of two courtyard houses, VII.27N and I.28N (pp. 50–53), can still be seen on Pound Lane.

*Above: A number of different types of lock and key have been found at Caerwent: the inhabitants of* Venta Silurum *were conscious of security. These are two examples of keys (Newport Museum and Art Gallery).*

The walls of the earlier dwellings were of timber-framed construction. The framing was filled with wattle and daub, plastered and limewashed — sometimes in colour — to protect it. Such buildings are usually identified during excavation by the holes for the uprights and the trenches in which they sat, the timbers having been withdrawn during demolition, or having long rotted away. Most of the later houses were well built, with walls of limestone intermingled with a small amount of Old Red Sandstone. Where the walls are fairly thick, they were probably carried up in stone throughout, but in some cases the walls may have been only a few courses high to raise a timber-framed structure off the damp ground. The external walls of most buildings would have been rendered and painted. It would appear that houses rarely had upper floors, but one house (XI.15S) had a cellar.

At first, ceramic tiles were used for roofing: they were of two kinds, the flanged *tegulae* and the semi-cylindrical *imbrices*, which covered the joints between rows of the *tegulae*. In the third and fourth centuries, however, stone slabs were employed; hexagonal in shape, they were nailed to a planked roof. The ridge of this type of roof was covered with shaped Bath Stone blocks and the gable-end often carried an ornamental finial in the form of a lantern.

At Caerwent, the only window opening to survive is in the cellar of XI.15S. To provide the necessary light in the best rooms, the windows would probably have been fairly large. Some would have been glazed, but Roman window glass had a bluish-green tint and was not completely transparent. Glazed or not, windows were often protected either by heavy wooden shutters or iron grilles, as can be seen at Herculaneum and Pompeii.

The position of doorways can be inferred from gaps in walls and in some cases the presence of stone door sills. Doors were normally pivoted rather than hung on hinges, and iron pivot shoes and sockets have survived. To protect property, doors could be locked, and there are several different types of lock and key.

Floors were simply of trodden earth, perhaps originally supporting wooden floorboards, or sometimes of concrete incorporating crushed tile (*opus signinum*), or of flagstones, but the principal rooms and corridors in the larger houses often had mosaic pavements. During the fourth century, the building of new houses, and alterations carried out on existing dwellings, provided the opportunity for the laying of new floors. Most of the Caerwent mosaics date to this period. In general, they are geometric in design, though representations of human and animal forms were sometimes attempted, as on the 'Seasons' pavement in Newport Museum and Art Gallery.

The walls and ceilings of rooms were plastered and often painted in bright colours. The most common form of wall decoration was a series of panels framed in contrasting colours and divided by vertical bands or pilasters. Some walls had more elaborate designs with figures and motifs. Those ceilings that were painted bore colourful designs that reflected the pattern of squares, hexagons, and circles on the mosaic floor below.

Establishing what individual rooms were used for is usually very difficult, for often only the foundations survive. It is sometimes possible to identify rooms, such as the kitchen, from artefactual remains, while the larger decorated rooms probably served as the main reception areas, such as the dining room (*triclinium*). Some of the principal rooms had the luxury of an underfloor heating system or hypocaust. Other rooms were probably warmed by braziers.

*Above: Walls and ceilings of finer rooms in Caerwent houses were plastered and often painted in bright colours. This fragment of painted wall plaster, depicting a girl's face, was found in a room at House XVI.2S in 1901 (Newport Museum and Art Gallery).*

*Left: A watercolour illustration showing part of a mosaic pavement found during excavations at House XI.15S in 1910 (Newport Museum and Art Gallery).*

*Left: A reconstruction of a 'typical' Romano-British dining room in a grand house of about AD 300 (Museum of London).*

*Above: An altar dedicated to the particularly British deity, Mars-Ocelus, found in House XII.16S. The inscription reads: 'To the God Mars Ocelus, Aelius Augustinus, optio [sub-centurion, no doubt from Caerleon], willingly and deservedly fulfilled his vow.'*

*Bottom left: A statue base with a dedication to the Rhenish god Mars-Lenus. Found in House XVIII.11S, the inscription reads: 'To the God Mars Lenus, otherwise Ocelus Vellaunus, and to the divinity of the Emperor. Marcus Nonius Romanus presented this [statue] at his own expense in recognition of the immunity from tax granted to his guild. On the tenth day before the Kalends of September, in the consulship of Glabrio and Homulus' (Newport Museum and Art Gallery).*

*Bottom right: The 1901 excavations in the yard of House XI.7S uncovered evidence for a domestic shrine. The deity was represented by this crude sandstone head (Newport Museum and Art Gallery).*

## Life of the Spirit

Excavations have revealed the sites of several religious buildings as well as a number of altars and statuettes. Religion in Roman Britain was a mixture of both native and imported ideas. Roman gods and goddesses, such as Jupiter, Mars, Minerva and Venus, were worshipped side by side with Celtic deities, which were usually concerned with the powers of nature. When native deities could be identified with their Roman equivalents there was often a fusion of beliefs; Mars-Ocelus, named on a small altar from Caerwent, is a good example. He was a particularly British if not a Silurian deity, being mentioned on only one other dedication, an altar from Carlisle. The Caerwent altar is of typical form, with a small hollow on top for the sacrificial fire. It would have been erected in response to the outcome of a vow to the god, possibly to ensure a victory, or recovery from disease, or some such event.

Another inscription on a statue base, which had been reused in building a wall of XVIII.11S, is a dedication to Mars-Lenus, a Rhenish god from the district of Trier. No doubt he was introduced to Caerwent either by legionaries or traders. He is equated with the local deity Ocelus Vellaunus ('the powerful') and the two gods must have been of a similar character. On top of the pedestal there are traces of the feet of the deity and a sacred bird.

The statue was a personal gift of Marcus Nonius Romanus to commemorate the immunity from taxation granted to his trade or religious guild, or — given the Rhenish connection — an association of foreigners; this took place on the tenth day before the Kalends of September, in the consulship of Glabrio and Homulus (23 August, AD 152). The inscription also, typically, includes mention of the divine spirit of the Roman emperor.

The imperial cult regarded emperors and members of their family as gods. In the early days of the conquest of Britain, a great temple was erected to the Emperor Claudius at Colchester. It was intended not only as a centre for the state religion but also a symbol of Roman domination. By focusing on the supreme ruler, the cult enabled the Romans to create a sense of unity throughout the empire.

The inhabitants of Caerwent worshipped their gods in a form of temple developed by Celtic peoples of the Roman Empire (pp. 45–46). Also, in many homes there would have been a small shrine with a figure of the favourite god who protected the family. Among the most popular in Britain were small figures in pottery or bronze of Venus, Mars and Mercury. At Caerwent, a small domestic shrine was uncovered in the yard of House XI.7S, which was probably a farm. The small square shrine had an open, balustraded front, and inside was a platform

reached by three steps, an offering table and a hearth used in the rituals. A crude sandstone head of a deity was found on the platform in the shrine. The Celts regarded the head as the seat of the soul, and here it was possibly being used as an element of ancestor worship. The shrine dates to the fourth century AD and was probably for the use of pagan farm workers, for it is likely that the family in the big house was Christian at this time. This would explain the siting of the shrine so far from the house.

Christians had been given the freedom to worship openly by the Emperor Constantine in 313, and there is evidence of a Christian community at *Venta Silurum*. A number of vessels was found in a large sealed urn which had been buried, in the late fourth century, level with the floor in a room of House IX.7N. One of these vessels was a pewter bowl on which a Christian symbol had been scratched. The chi-rho monogram represents the first two Greek letters of Christ's name. It has been suggested that these vessels, carefully segregated, were used in the early Christian supper known as the *agape* ('friendly affection'), held after the Eucharist at the invitation of some well-to-do member of the community at his own house for his poorer fellows.

There is no sign of a purpose-built church within the walls, but the first places of Christian worship were located within houses, part adapted for just this use. One such possibility at Caerwent is House V.22N, the northern rooms of which bear resemblance, in their altered ground plan, to what might be expected of a house-church. A nave can be identified, with an easterly apse, a vestibule or narthex, and sacristies.

The cemeteries of Caerwent remain one of the largest gaps in our knowledge of the Roman town. Cremation was the custom until the later second or third century. Several cremation burials have been found within the town walls, beneath later buildings; suggesting that the earlier cemeteries were built over as the town expanded. In the third and fourth centuries, changes in religious thought saw the reintroduction of inhumation burial, but at Caerwent the later cemeteries are largely unknown. Two cemeteries of the early medieval period have been discovered; that outside the east gate may be late fourth century in origin (p. 29).

*Above: A ritual sacrifice portrayed on the Bridgeness distance slab from the Antonine Wall. The form of the ceremony is typical of Roman religion and shows how altars were used (© The Trustees of the National Museums of Scotland).*

*Left: One of the vessels found in a large sealed urn in House IX.7N in 1906 was a pewter bowl. Scratched on the base of the bowl was a Christian symbol, the chi-rho monogram, representing the first two letters of Christ's name (Newport Museum and Art Gallery).*

*Venta Silurum was sited on a slight rise in an area of prime agricultural land. Originally unfortified, the town acquired its first defences, in the form of an earthen rampart topped by a timber palisade, in the later years of the second century AD. The stone wall that still surrounds the town was built in front of the earlier earthen bank probably in the closing years of the third century, and the towers were added to strengthen the defences around AD 350.*

# The Town Defences

Although the boundaries of *Venta Silurum* may have been demarcated at its foundation, the early settlement was not fortified. Not only were defences unnecessary because of the military situation, but also they could be obtained only by permission from the governor, or even the emperor, who, in normal circumstances, would have been unlikely to grant the request for fear of a native rebellion. Many of the larger towns, including *Venta*, acquired defences piecemeal during the later years of the second century. These early fortifications, which were either a response to some emergency or possibly in anticipation of a crisis, took the form of earthworks that could be erected cheaply, quickly and without the need for skilled masons.

At Caerwent, the earthen rampart, lying on a cobbled surface for stability, was as much as 30 feet (9m) wide and survives, in places, to a height of 6 feet (1.8m). The earth for the bank was obtained from a V-shaped ditch excavated immediately in front. On top of the bank there would have been a vertical palisade of stout timbers and a broad rampart walkway. The form and appearance of the gates at this time are unknown. However, it is possible that the extant stone gatehouses were built at the same time as the earthen defences or they may have replaced timber gateways during the life of the rampart. Such an arrangement is known at the Roman towns of Cirencester (*Corinium*) and St Albans (*Verulamium*).

Later, a stone wall was built in front of the original earthen bank. Despite several excavations, the precise

date of the construction of the town wall is uncertain, but opinion now favours the late third century, like so many other town walls in Britain. This situation reflects the changing pattern of military strategy and growing insecurity as a result of increased piratical raids at this time. As well as providing protection for the administration, individual wealth and supplies of food, the wall would also have been a source of civic pride and status. In places the wall still stands to a height of 17 feet (5m). Originally, it would have been up to 25 feet (7.5m) high, with either a single- or possibly a double-ditch system in front.

There were gates in all four sides of the town. The largest were the east and west gates, placed nearly centrally in the respective walls, on the line of the main thoroughfare. They were flanked by square towers, which projected both behind and in front of the wall, while their probable width suggests that they had two carriageways. The south and north gates, both single-arched openings, were neither centrally placed nor in opposing positions. Their staggered placing (see the plan on the inside back cover) was probably owing to the position of existing buildings and roads at the time the fortifications were erected.

Subsequently, the defences were further strengthened by the addition of external towers, six on the south wall and at least five on the north. The arrangement of the towers at Caerwent is distinctly irregular, and they are completely absent from the east and west sides. A coin hoard — found in the builders' debris of the north-west tower — indicates that the towers were constructed at a date very close to AD 349–50. The inner ditch had to be refilled and recut slightly further out in the area in

*An artist's impression of the west gate at Caerwent in the early fourth century AD, showing a section through the defences of the town. The stone gatehouses of the town may have been built at the same time as the earthen ramparts or constructed later to replace timber structures. Information on the defensive sequence has been compiled from several excavations (Illustration by John Banbury, 1992).*

*In design, the towers added to the walls at Caerwent in the mid-fourth century closely resemble those to be found at the Roman fort at Cardiff, itself newly built in the late third century. This view shows the early twentieth-century reconstruction of the north gate at Cardiff.*

*To judge from the amount of late Roman military equipment that has been found at Caerwent, an army garrison may have been maintained in the town in the fourth century. The* plumbata *(a barbed projectile) seen here, with a modern replica, is one of those late weapons (Newport Museum and Art Gallery; replica: National Museum of Wales).*

front of the towers to allow for their construction. In design, the towers resembled those to be found at the Roman fort at Cardiff, which was probably also built in the late third century. It seems likely that the towers would have been manned by archers, possibly belonging to an army garrison. From the top of the towers, the archers could cover the ground at the base of the wall if the enemy approached too close. Alternatively, it has been suggested that they housed arrow-firing artillery (*ballistae*). By this time, a double-ditched system certainly existed in front of the wall. There is no evidence, however, that *Venta* ever came under attack.

## The End of Venta Silurum

By the late third century, the Roman military dispositions in Wales were concerned more with external threats of seaborne raiders descending upon the region from Ireland than with the possibility of tribal uprisings. The withdrawal of the Second Augustan Legion from Caerleon, towards the end of the third century, created the additional need to reorganize the defences to combat this threat from the sea.

*Evidence for a considerable amount of new building, such as the substantial courtyard house (I.28N), shows that the first half of the fourth century was a time of prosperity for Caerwent. House I.28N had several hypocausts, one shown here, and mosaics.*

*The south gate, which accommodated only a single carriageway, was probably little used by traffic. It was eventually blocked at a late stage of the town's Roman history.*

A series of late Roman defended sites was built around the western British coastline, enabling patrols to police the main estuaries along which the Irish might travel. Forts were established at Cardiff and Lancaster. There were also defensive roles for pre-existing forts at Caernarfon, Chester, Loughor and Neath. An army garrison may also have been maintained at Caerwent itself in the fourth century, to judge from the amount of late military equipment and coinage that has come to light.

The growing insecurity in the countryside appears to have resulted in the gradual running down of farms, with access to markets becoming more difficult and profits declining. Doubtless, some farmers and their families affected by the hostilities sought the safety of *Venta Silurum*, while others appear to have taken refuge behind the defences of several Iron Age hillforts. The first half of the fourth century was a time of great prosperity for Caerwent, to judge from the considerable amount of new building undertaken and the more lavish decoration of houses.

With the construction of the town wall, followed by the addition of the towers, the inhabitants of *Venta* probably felt safe from attack. At a later stage, it was thought necessary to restrict access in and out of the town still further by blocking both the north and south gates.

The dismantling of the remaining military forces stationed in Wales had until recent years been attributed to Magnus Maximus, a general of Spanish origin — who reappears later in Welsh legend as Macsen Wledig. In AD 383, the popular Maximus was elected emperor by the army in Britain, and it is widely held that he took many troops to fight on the

*A gold coin of Magnus Maximus, the usurper emperor (AD 383–88). He was finally defeated by Theodosius and later executed at Aquileia, Italy (National Museum of Wales).*

*Right: Holyhead, Anglesey, was the site of a late Roman naval base. It is one of a number of defended sites built around the western British coast to discourage raiders from across the Irish Sea. There was also a Roman signal station on top of nearby Caer y Tŵr, shown here.*

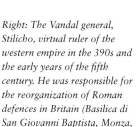

*Right: The Vandal general, Stilicho, virtual ruler of the western empire in the 390s and the early years of the fifth century. He was responsible for the reorganization of Roman defences in Britain (Basilica di San Giovanni Baptista, Monza, Italy/Bridgeman Art Library).*

*Above: Metalwork and coins from Caerwent suggest activity of some kind from the seventh century through to the Norman Conquest. The finds include this silver penny of Æthelred II (d. 1016), minted at Lincoln in 991–97 (Newport Museum and Art Gallery).*

*Far right: Early medieval material from Caerwent included this group of pins. Note the spiral-headed type of the seventh century and the Viking type with a 'knobbed ring' of the late ninth or tenth century (Newport Museum and Art Gallery).*

Continent where he overthrew the Emperor Gratian (AD 367–83), and retained power over Gaul and Britain until AD 388. However, coins found during excavations at Caernarfon (*Segontium*) point to a continued military occupation at this key fort until AD 395. A signal station on the very top of Holyhead Mountain has also produced coinage of the same late date. The presence of Roman forces in north Wales at this late period may be explained by the need to protect the copper workings on Anglesey and, perhaps, the silver-bearing lead along the Flintshire coast.

There is no comparable activity at military sites in south Wales at this late date. Caerwent, however, has yielded numerous coins of the last decade of the fourth century, of the house of Theodosius, the latest to arrive in this country from the mints of Gaul and Italy. Such late coins have been found at other sites on both sides of the Severn estuary, indicating the importance of the waterway in guarding the approach to Cirencester (*Corinium*), the capital of *Britannia Prima*, and to the rich countryside of the Cotswolds. It is noteworthy that in south Wales, unlike the north, we can trace events further with the presence of coins of Honorius, who became emperor in AD 393.

This late coinage may have come in as army pay, and may link Severnside with the reorganization of Roman defences in Britain by Stilicho, the great Vandal general of Honorius, in the late 390s. Some of these late Roman forces doubtless collected at Caerwent to defend against piratical attacks by seaborne raiders. This was a short-lived arrangement, and within a few years Wales had been stripped of the last troops.

The end of *Venta* is not well understood. By the later fourth century, the town had probably started to contract, with House I.28N, for example, abandoned at this time. However, life appears to have continued in some form into the fifth century, but by then much of the town was in a ruinous state. Some of the Theodosian hoards, to judge from the wear on the coins, may have been deposited or discarded as late as AD 425, by which time they had probably become valueless.

By the early sixth century, the kingdom of Gwent had come into existence, and it has always been claimed that its title was derived from the name of the town. Little is known about the early medieval period at Caerwent, and no structural evidence can be firmly attributed to that time. Burials of this period have, however, been found inside the town, adjacent to the present church, and outside the east gate. In 1910, the Vicarage Orchard, just outside the east gate, was explored and thirty interments were discovered. Further excavation of this cemetery in 1973 produced 118 burials, some of which have been dated, using the radiocarbon method, to between the fourth and ninth centuries. The burials were aligned in an east–west direction, and the most important graves were stone lined. There appears to have been a specific area in the cemetery for children and adolescents. The size and form of the cemetery inside the town are unclear, but over 150 burials have been recorded. Some of the graves respect Roman building lines, and probably belong to the early medieval period, while others cut across demolished Roman walls and may be considerably later.

The significance of these early medieval cemeteries is unclear. They could indicate settlement — either secular or ecclesiastical — within or close to the town, or simply the continued use of the site by the surrounding population for burial.

Metalwork and coins from the site also imply activity of some kind from the seventh century to the Norman Conquest. However, when the Normans arrived, they chose the strategically important site of Chepstow — which guards the river crossing near the mouth of the Wye — to build their castle. At Caerwent, they threw up only a small castle mound (motte) in the south-east corner of the town (p. 35). Chepstow developed as a flourishing port during the medieval period, whereas Caerwent, with only a small number of cottages and farms within the walls, returned largely to pasture. When John Leland visited the site about 1540, there were only sixteen or seventeen newly built small houses for husbandmen within and about the walls.

# St Tatheus

The 'Life of Tatheus' (*Vita Tathei*), probably written about 1125–40, tells how the saint came from Ireland and, after performing a series of miracles, was given the site of the Roman town by the local king, Caradog ab Ynyr, whose residence it was. Tatheus founded there a monastic settlement, and King Caradog moved out to a site which can be identified as Portskewett, just over 2 miles (3.5 km) south-east of Caerwent. The basis of the record is no doubt sound and would relate to the sixth century.

This tale of St Tatheus has led to some curious claims. In 1910 the Vicarage Orchard, just outside the east gate, opposite the site of the Burton Homes, was trenched. Some thirty skeletons were found, most disposed about another that lay in a cist of stone slabs manifestly of post-Roman date, because it was constructed across the ruined wall of a Roman building. This led a number of people to believe that it was the burial of St Tatheus himself. The remains were removed with great ceremony in 1912 from the cemetery to the south aisle of St Stephen's, the parish church. The coffin was laid to rest under a fine slab bearing an elaborate Latin inscription. Others rightly dismissed the whole affair, for there are several flaws in the case for these bones being those of St Tatheus. Firstly, the stone cist grave was, in fact, not unique, for unknown to the excavators three cist burials had already been recorded from the cemetery in 1855; many more graves, some in similar cists, were to be excavated in 1973.

Apparently unknown to all concerned, there was also a record that in 1235 a gift was made to Tewkesbury Abbey of various relics, including 'three bones of St Tatheus, who is buried at Caerwent'. How these bones were identified as those of the saint is unknown.

The tradition also influenced V. E. Nash-Williams in his interpretation of a small structure that had been built over the demolished west end of the exercise hall of the public baths, not far from the parish church. At the time of the excavation, in 1923, he considered it to have been a small Christian church associated with St Tatheus. This interpretation has now been dismissed.

*The stone cist burial, discovered in 1910, and wrongly identified as that of the sixth-century saint, Tatheus.*

*A bronze penannular brooch of the fifth or sixth century from the cemetery outside the east gate (National Museum of Wales).*

# A Tour of Roman Venta Silurum

There is much to remind the visitor of Caerwent's Roman past. Within the magnificent defences, there are the foundations of shops and houses and a Romano-Celtic temple on view. At the very heart of the Roman town, much of the *forum-basilica* has been uncovered for display, and this is the only site in Britain where such a building can be seen. The street running through the village lies more or less directly on the line of the main Roman road, but it was much wider then than it is today.

The church in the centre of the village is also well worth a visit, for it houses some important Roman items. Within the porch you will find the original Paulinus inscription (p. 11), together with the altar to Mars-Ocelus (p. 22). Built into the west wall of the south aisle are several sculptured stones, which may be elements of a floral frieze that once adorned the public baths, and also a pottery urn containing a cremation. On the floor, near the chancel arch, there is a fragment of mosaic found in 1910.

Most visitors to this pleasant village will probably start their tour from the car park. Panel 1 provides a general introduction and a key to the tour followed in this guide, though other routes are possible using the footpaths shown on the plan below. The location of further panels is noted in the text and on the plan below. Close by, in the open-fronted barn, you will find more information about Roman Caerwent. From the car park, make your way to the site of the west gate.

*Opposite: A view along the well-preserved southern defences of the Roman town. Some of the walls stand up to 17 feet (5m) high, though originally they may have reached 25 feet (7.5m).*

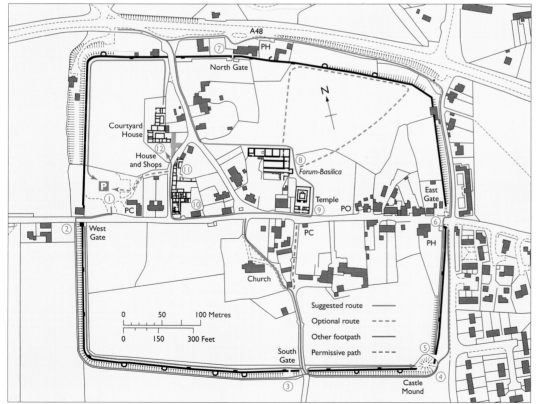

**Access Information**
Much of the site is flat or has gentle gradients. There are numerous gates and few benches or shelter. There are narrow pavements on the public roads at the eastern end of the village and no pavements elsewhere. There are public toilets on the road near the temple.

*Above: A second-century enamelled brooch in the form of a running hare found at Caerwent (Newport Museum and Art Gallery).*

# The Town Wall

Caerwent has the best preserved defences of any Roman town in Britain. The total circuit of the wall slightly exceeds a mile (1.6km). They are best viewed at the south gate [Panel 3], or at the south-east corner of the town [Panel 4]. You may use the suggested tour route from the west gate, or the footpaths marked on the map on p. 31. The footpath through the churchyard to the south gate crosses grass and a stone stile. This can be bypassed by the smooth and gently sloping permissive path along the farm track. Beyond this, the lane is rough grass with ruts and slopes more steeply. The west gate is accessed via a stone stile that can be bypassed using the accessible gate further along the road.

## The West Gate and Wall [Panel 2]

*Below: All that remains of the west gate is part of the south wall of the south tower, and the base of the guardroom. From the gate to the south-west corner of the town, the wall stands to an average height of 10 feet (3m).*

*Below right: The distinctive herringbone pattern of the core of the west wall.*

Once the defences were raised, the town could have been entered by any one of four gates, the largest of which were in the east and west walls, on the main road through the town (see p. 25). Both probably had double-arched carriageways, flanked by square towers which projected both in front of and behind the town wall. Little of the west gateway now survives [Panel 2].

On the south side of the road (just inside the stile) is part of the south wall of the tower, with a course of large sandstone blocks in its lower part, and the

masonry floor of the guardroom. The wall of the gate-tower is not bonded into the town wall, but it is uncertain what this signifies. It has been suggested that it merely indicates that the gate was built by a separate gang of workmen, if it is contemporary with the town wall, but it is also possible that the gatehouse was built during the life of the earthen rampart. Only further excavation will resolve this question. Most of the gate structure lies beneath the road and the cottage to the north. The ditch was interrupted in front of the gate to allow traffic and pedestrians in and out of the town.

The best view of this stretch of the defences is obtained from the path on the outside of the wall, towards the south-west corner. This low-level path is grassed and uneven. The footpath at rampart level is gently undulating grass with benches. There are steps at the west and south gates.

From the west gate to the south-west corner, the wall stands to an average height of some 10 feet (3m), but in places it is still over 17 feet (5m) high. The wall, built mostly of limestone, is backed by an earthen bank, which in part was made up of the partially dismantled earlier earthwork. There is no trace of the wall-walk that must have run along the top of the wall; but it has been estimated that the wall, including the parapet, probably stood up to 25 feet (7.5m). The wall is 10 feet (3m) thick at its base, but is gradually reduced by a series of offsets on its inner face (not now visible) to about 6 feet 6 inches (2m) wide. Apart from a slightly projecting plinth course, the outer face of the wall was originally vertical.

The method of construction can clearly be seen in this stretch of the wall. The builders began by laying rows, front and back, of facing stones of roughly hammer-dressed limestone blocks. Then, the core was filled with pieces of limestone bedded roughly on edge followed by a slurry of lime mortar; the whole structure was raised course by course. This method of construction resulted in the herringbone pattern of the core so clearly visible here. The wall was built in sections by different gangs of workmen. The breaks where one gang ended its operations and another started have been well disguised on the outer face, but on the inner, which was largely hidden by the bank, they are fairly easy to see. The section of wall south of the west gate was built in two or possibly three sections. It appears that no towers were built on this side of the town.

Two ditches have been found beyond the wall. Between the wall and the inner ditch there was a narrow berm, 5 feet (1.5m) wide, for stability. The bottom of the slight slope at this point more or less marks the inner lip of the ditch. The inner ditch was some 44 feet (13.5m) wide and a maximum of 8 feet (2.5m) deep, and was probably dug or recut when the wall was constructed. The outer ditch, which took the form of a shallow U shape, was 24 feet (7.3m) wide and 6 feet (1.8m) deep. It was separated from the inner ditch by an interval of some 26 feet (8m), but there is now no surface indication of the outer ditch at this point. It was either dug when the wall was built, or it may have been a later addition to the defensive system. The defences as a whole presented a formidable obstacle. At the end of this stretch, you will see that the south-west corner is rounded off, as is usual in Roman defensive work.

> Continue along the outside of the wall towards Panel 3, located next to the south gate.

# The South Gate, Wall and Towers [Panel 3]

The south wall is not completely straight, but bows outwards slightly in its middle section. It stands in places to an impressive height of 17 feet (5m), and is

of similar construction to the west wall. Breaks found, during excavation, in the inner face of the wall show it to have been built in fourteen sections; these breaks are not visible in the outer face. At various places along the wall rows of putlog holes can be seen; these were used for securing timber staging from which the masons could work during construction. A trench excavated in 1925 across the two large ditches showed that they were roughly the same dimensions, about 30 feet (9m) wide and 7 to 8 feet (2m) deep.

The remains of six hollow towers, spaced at irregular intervals, project from the south wall. In external plan, they are all five sided. By looking closely you will see that the towers are not bonded into the town wall, which demonstrates that they are later additions to strengthen the defences. The inner ditch had to be refilled and then recut in front of the towers to allow their construction. It is possible that the outer ditch, some 27 feet (8m) from the inner one, was cut at the same time.

A point to look for in the first tower you approach (nearest the south-west corner) is the small postern door in the east side, which was later blocked by masonry.

*The best preserved of the six hollow towers that were added to the south wall in the middle of the fourth century AD. There would have been two wooden floors above the ground floor and a platform, probably of timber, at wall-walk level would have given sentries a good line of sight along the walls.*

*Right: A reconstruction of one of the Caerwent towers as it may have appeared in the later fourth century. It is shown manned by guards, including an archer (Illustration by John Banbury, 1992).*

*Below: In the late Roman period, both the north and south gates into Caerwent were blocked. This view of the south gate shows the blocking wall. The moulded imposts — the large flat blocks of stone either side of the gate above which the masonry begins to curve — of the gate arch are clearly visible. When the gate was blocked, the culvert underneath — which drained the public baths — was rebuilt at a higher level. This implies that the baths were still in use at this late stage of the town's history.*

The fourth tower from the west is the best preserved, and stands to a height of over 13 feet (4m). Internal joist holes suggest that there were two wooden floors besides the ground floor. The top platform, at the same level as the wall-walk, was probably of timber (see reconstruction drawing) and would have provided sentries with a good sight along the wall. The lower floors must have been reached by ladders through trapdoors. They would have had no natural light and little headroom, and must have been used as stores.

The south gate (situated just before the fenced farm track) lay at the end of the street to the east of the public baths [Panel 3]. The gate consisted of a single-arched passageway and was built separately from the south wall. The piers, which carried the inner and outer arches (better seen from the rear), project considerably in front of the external face of the wall and to a lesser extent behind its internal face. The arches may have supported an overhead chamber or merely carried the wall-walk over the gate. Both sides of the passage were originally recessed so that the heavy doors at the front could swing back. The road passing through the gate was made up of stones and iron clinker, and beneath it was a slab-lined culvert (still to be seen at the lowest point in the centre).

At a later date, the gate was blocked with two well-constructed walls, one built at the rear of the gate and the other on line with the front of the town wall; the gap between the two being filled with rubble and mortar. At the same time the front of the gate was partially dismantled, so as to remove any cover that might have been useful to an attacker. A new culvert (also visible) was built at a higher level passing through the masonry blocking.

> **At this point you can climb the nearby steps to view the back of the Roman gate.**

From here you can see the inner arch partially preserved above the moulded imposts, together with the later blocking wall. It can also be seen that the interior level is now much higher than that outside the town walls, a situation that is often brought about by the building of defences around a settlement. It is, however, more noticeable here because of the natural slope of the ground.

After viewing the south gate, cross the farm track using the accessible gates. From here either climb the steps and walk along the top of the undulating grass bank above the wall as far as the east gate, or continue along the low-level path until you reach the motte, or castle mound [Panel 4]. The best views of the Roman defences can be gained from Panel 4. Steps lead to the top of the rampart and Panel 5.

At the higher level, you will gain an excellent idea of the splendid view of the countryside that would have been obtained from the wall-walk, and you will appreciate how difficult it would have been for anyone to approach unobserved. At intervals (approximately 200 feet, 60m) along the back of the wall there are stone projections, the inner side of the wall being carried up to its full thickness instead of being reduced by a series of offsets. These have previously been called 'counterforts', but technically this is incorrect for they do not support or strengthen the wall. It is possible that they mark the positions of wooden

steps up to the wall-walk, though it has been suggested that they may have been platforms for arrow-firing *ballistae*.

> Steps beside the castle mound give access to the low-level route and Panel 4.

## The Castle Mound [Panel 4]

In the south-east corner of the town there is a large motte, or castle mound. This is all that remains of a small earth-and-timber castle, which was built by the Normans towards the end of the eleventh century. The Norman invaders reused the already existing defences, and the mound was protected on two sides by the Roman ditches. There are traces of a ditch having been dug to protect it on the north side where the ground was marshy. It also appears that they demolished part of the Roman wall on either side of the mound to isolate the fortification. The current profile reflects recent repairs to damage caused by weathering and slippage.

*One of the stone projections on the inner side of the south wall. These projections may mark the positions of wooden steps up to the wall-walk, or may have served as platforms for arrow-firing* ballistae.

*The Norman motte was raised in the south-east corner of the Roman defences in the late eleventh century.*

*Above: The east wall running towards the surviving fragment of the southern tower of the east gate. The gate, one of the two principal entries into the Roman town, probably had a double-arched carriageway.*

*In 1912, during the construction of the Burton Homes almshouses, a curious Roman structure was revealed. It is uncertain whether it was a temple or a monumental tomb. This photograph shows a portion of the outer circular wall of the structure during excavations (National Museum of Wales).*

# The East Gate and Wall [Panel 6]

At rampart level, after passing the castle mound, you will find Panel 5. From here, you can gain a good view of the large unexcavated areas of the town, represented by the earthworks in the fields to the south-east of the church. Continue along the top of the defences to the east gate [Panel 6]. Alternatively, visitors using the low-level route may continue as far as the east gate. Note, however, at the low level there is no access to the road at the east gate; visitors should return to the south gate to rejoin the main tour route (see plan on p. 31).

The town wall on the east side is bowed outwards, having its maximum projection just south of the east gate. There are two stone projections on the inside face of the wall to the south of the east gate; these are rather more than 200 feet (60m) apart. As on the west, there are no external towers on this side of the town.

All that remains of the east gate [Panel 6] is the inner angle of the tower on the south side of the modern (and Roman) road. The gate-tower is not bonded into the town wall. Although the plan of the tower is incomplete, like that of the west gate, it was probably square, and would have projected forward from the front line of the town wall. The tower had a course of large sandstone blocks near its base. From below, you will see that the modern road surface is 4 feet (1.2m) below the level of the east gate; the road having been lowered to reduce the gradient for traffic. As already mentioned, this was one of the two principal gates of the town, joined by the main highway. It probably had a double-arched carriageway, but the width is unknown, for all traces of the gate structure on the northern side have disappeared.

At Panel 6, either turn left below the wall and return along the main street towards the temple and *forum-basilica* (pp. 38–46), or if you wish to see the northern half of the defensive system from the outside, cross the main road and continue along the road outside the east wall.

The wall to the north of the east gate, once again, clearly illustrates the method of construction (pp. 32–33). The east side of the town is almost 100 feet (30m) shorter than the west, for the north-east corner of the town is pulled in, so as to take advantage of the high ground and avoid a marshy depression that existed in Roman times. To the east of the lane are the Burton Homes, underneath which lies part of a curious Roman structure. During the erection of these almshouses in 1912, some workmen, digging to find stone for the garden wall, unearthed a length of Roman wall. A rapid rescue excavation revealed an octagonal building surrounded by a circular wall, with an overall diameter of 130 feet (40m). It has been interpreted as an octagonal temple set within a sacred enclosure (*temenos*), but the possibility that it was a monumental tomb cannot be discounted.

## The North Gate and Wall [Panel 7]

> Turn left into the pedestrianized lane before the bypass. This low-level route along the northern defences is level or gently sloping, without steps.

This lane follows the line of the outer ditch at this point. The inner edge of the ditch lies approximately 75 feet (23m) from the north wall and, overall, it would have been some 30 feet (9m) wide. The north wall is the least well preserved of all the walls, having suffered greatly from stone robbing and building encroachment; it rarely survives to a height greater than 6 feet (1.8m). Where not exposed, the line of the wall is marked by the innermost hedgerow.

In places on the north side, the earlier earthen bank was entirely removed before the wall was built. This was probably done to allow the wall to stand on the line of the bank, and thus have a more commanding position. In some places, therefore, the bank as seen today is not the original earthen rampart as elsewhere, but was newly piled up behind the wall after the latter was built. The sites of five towers are preserved, but except for the north-west tower only the foundations and lowest courses survive.

> The north gate [Panel 7] stands immediately to the west (right) and just to the rear of the public house, also called The North Gate.

Like the south gate, and for the same reason (pp. 25, 34), the north gate is not centrally placed in the town wall. Directly opposite the gate, the ditch was reduced

in width to 10 feet (3m), presumably for the ease of bridging. In plan, the gate is very similar to that of the south, except in this case there is no forward projection beyond the line of the town wall. The passage of the gate was 10 feet (3m) wide, and the sides are recessed between the inner and outer arches, with the space serving to take the gate when open. At some time, the arches were dismantled, but on the west side of the gate the moulded imposts which carried them are still in position. Also still in place, level with the front of the gate, are the blocks of sandstone that contained the round iron sockets for the pivots of the wooden doors.

Probably in the late Roman period, the gate was blocked by a roughly built wall. The masonry in this blocking was mainly reused material, including a column base at the rear, either from a demolished or ruined building. This blocking was carried out when the gate was already in a ruinous state, for the wall was partially built over the end of the east pier. For access, the postern that survives today was left in the blocking. A large sandstone block served as the lintel to this doorway. Such a block must either have been the cornice from a window or door of a Roman building, or a coping stone.

> Continue along the path beside the bypass, crossing the lane on your left, towards the north-west tower. The remains lie in a large compound, which is private land, though the tower can be seen from the entrance. The north-west defences can also be viewed from inside the Roman town at the end of the tour (p. 53).

*A view of the north gate, situated beside and to the rear of 'The North Gate' public house. Like the south gate, the single carriageway here was blocked in the late Roman period, but a postern was constructed to allow pedestrian access.*

*The remains of the north-west tower. The presence of the so-called King's Pool may indicate that the Roman ditches held water at this point.*

The north-west tower survives to a height of 8 feet (2.4m) at the junction with the town wall. The external plan of the tower is five sided. The D-shaped internal foundation offset may have been designed to support a wooden floor; a similar offset has been noted in most of the other towers. Excavation of the tower, in 1971, revealed small patches of flush pointing, with a fine-textured white lime mortar, on the town wall where the tower abutted it and where deposits had accumulated against the face. Of greater significance was the discovery of a coin hoard, which indicated that this tower was in the process of being constructed in AD 349–50.

At this point, there are clear surface indications of both the inner and outer ditches skirting the town wall. The existence of the so-called King's Pool may indicate that the ditches held water at this point in Roman times.

> Return towards the main street via the lane between the north-west tower and the north gate for about 250 yards (225m). Just after you have passed Vine Tree Cottage, turn left through an accessible metal gate and proceed to the site of the *forum-basilica* along a gravel path [Panel 8].

# The Forum-Basilica [Panel 8]

At the centre of the town's public life, the *forum-basilica* (marketplace and civic hall) appropriately occupied the whole central building block (*Insula VIII*), north of the main street. The *basilica* would have towered over the surrounding shops and houses. Despite the immense size of the building, 260 feet (80m) north to south and 182 feet (56m) east to west, it is small compared with those of some other tribal capitals.

The site was first explored in 1907 and 1909, when an almost complete plan of the building was recovered, although there was no firm indication as to when it was first erected. In 1987, excavations began to uncover parts of the building for display and to unravel its structural history. The work has now been completed and the northern end of the *forum* and much of the *basilica* have been uncovered for display.

In the late first century BC, Marcus Vitruvius, a Roman architect and engineer, wrote in general about *fora-basilicae* in his famous treatise

*Below right: A view of the excavated portion of the* forum-basilica *complex from the south. The paved area in the foreground is part of the* forum *piazza and the* basilica *lies beyond.*

*Below: A group of workmen engaged in the first excavations of the* forum-basilica *in 1907 (National Museum of Wales).*

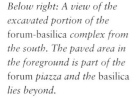

*De Architectura.* Some of the features and functions that he describes have been recognized in the Caerwent complex.

The *forum*, a rectangular open marketplace surrounded on three sides by ranges of rooms (see reconstruction drawing, pp. 40–41), was entered from the main street through an archway. Caerwent House (see adjacent plan) lies just to the east of the original entrance and is built on the south-east corner of the *forum*, covering the shops. The paved piazza provided space for temporary stalls to be set up on market days. The ranges of rooms, which were set behind a covered colonnade, served as shops, taverns and offices. Above these, to balance the lofty splendour of the *basilica*, there may have been a second storey, perhaps with a balcony and more rooms. The ground-floor shops each consisted of a single room, with a large open front, which could be closed with wooden shutters. On the east side the shops opened on to the piazza, whereas those on the south looked on to the main street. By contrast, the west wing, originally seems to have been a single long hall with a small office at one end.

Only one shop [**A**], in the north-eastern corner of the *forum*, is displayed. For much of its history, it may have been used as a snack bar. A masonry hearth, on which meals could have been cooked and drinks warmed, is still visible in the north-east corner. Gaming counters and personal items such as tweezers, nail cleaners and ear scrapers were found scattered within the shop area. They may have fallen between gaps in wooden floorboards. Part of the covered portico, which surrounded the *forum*, can also be seen at this point.

The fourth side of the *forum*, opposite the main entrance, was closed by the *basilica*. Access to the *basilica* was gained by steps — some of which survive — stretching the entire width of the *forum* piazza. The *basilica* had an open colonnaded façade, marked now only by its front wall, for all traces of the columns have long since disappeared. There were also doors at either end of the south aisle giving access from the side streets. That on the east side was fronted by a monumental archway, supported on massive blocks of Sudbrook sandstone (still visible) with a principal arch arranged parallel to the entrance. There were two opposing smaller arches set on the north and south sides allowing pedestrians direct access to the side of the *basilica*.

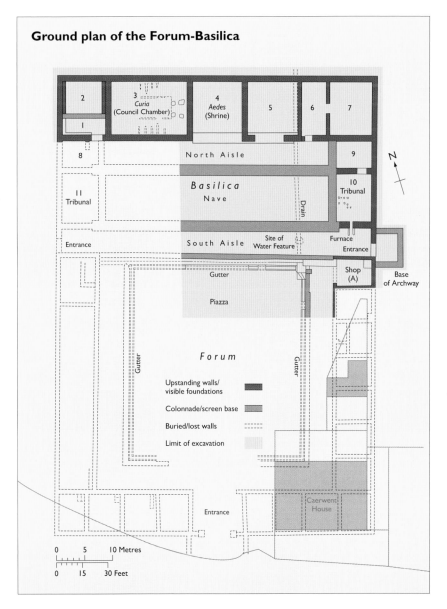

*Left: The* forum *was surrounded on three sides by shops, taverns and offices set behind a covered colonnade. The shops, with a wide open frontage, would have been similar to the cloth merchant's shop shown in this Italian relief of the first century AD (Museo della Civilta Romana, Rome/Bridgeman Art Library).*

*This reconstruction of the forum-basilica gives an impression of the complex during the second century. This was the centre of both commercial and public life within Roman Caerwent (Illustration by John Banbury, 1992).*

In plan, the *basilica* comprises the great hall and a rear range of rooms and chambers. Some of the walls stood, even before excavation, as much as 6 feet (1.8m) above ground level, having been incorporated into early nineteenth-century farm buildings (which have now been removed). The external walls of the *basilica*, and indeed those of the *forum* as well, were thickly rendered and painted off white. The roofs were entirely of tile in the original build, but later, towards the end of the third century, some were replaced with sandstone slabs.

The great hall comprised, as is generally the case, a nave and two aisles divided by colonnades supporting a clerestory like that of a great church, architecturally its lineal descendant. The walls that carried the great stone columns were massive, with foundations 6 feet (1.8m) deep, though unfortunately they bear no traces of the positions of the columns. However, a sufficient number of architectural fragments have been recovered to show that the columns were of the Corinthian style, carved from local sandstone, and that they rose to a height of

about 30 feet (9.2m). Allowing for an entablature, clerestory and the roof, the *basilica* could not have stood less than 65 feet (20m) high. The great hall would have been used for large public meetings and ceremonies, and perhaps by businessmen and merchants.

The chambers [10 and 11], at either end of the nave, probably served as tribunals for the local magistrates to hear civil cases. Only the governor of the province, or an appointed deputy, had the right to impose the death penalty, and *Venta Silurum*

may well have been designated an assize town for such capital cases to be heard. It is possible, therefore, that the trial of the two Caerleon martyrs, Julius and Aaron, may have taken place here in the third century. The men, probably soldiers, having been condemned as Christians, may have been taken back to Caerleon for execution and burial.

Only the eastern tribunal [10] is on view. It was originally separated from the main body of the hall by a stone screen, the slabs of which were held in a shallow groove cut into the row of sandstone blocks at the front of the tribunal. At a later stage, this was replaced by a wooden screen and double doors, which are marked by square sockets and bolt-holes. The block at the centre of the doorway shows traces of considerable wear with the passage of feet. There is also an entrance from the north aisle and the threshold stone can still be seen. In its latest form, the tribunal was heated by a hypocaust, perhaps after the demolition of the great hall. Some of the stone pillars that supported the raised floor of the hypocaust survive in place and the furnace was located in the south aisle, effectively blocking the side entrance.

*Above: This fragment of brick from the* forum-basilica *records a list of names with tally marks that probably relate to the production of bricks used in the construction (National Museum of Wales).*

*Below: The remains of the* basilica *seen from its eastern entrance. In the foreground is chamber 10, which probably served as a tribunal. In its latest form, the room was heated by a hypocaust and some of the stone pillars that supported the raised floor and the slabs of the furnace are still visible.*

*Above: Excavation of the* basilica *revealed the box drain running beneath its floor. Massive blocks of sandstone, some weighing more than a ton, were used for the sides and to cap the drain. The semicircular hole in one of the capstones probably marks the spot of a water feature (National Museum of Wales).*

*The rear range of rooms in the* basilica *provided office accommodation for the tribal administration. Writing implements such as these* styli *would have been used on wooden tablets coated with wax. Seal boxes were used with wax to secure the tablets on other documents (Newport Museum and Art Gallery).*

Beneath the floor of the *basilica* there was a box drain, which carried away rainwater that had collected in the gutters surrounding the *forum* piazza; several blocks of the stone gutter survive. The gutters emptied into the box drain in the north-east corner of the *forum*. Massive blocks of sandstone, some weighing in excess of a ton, were used for the sides and capping of the drain, while the base was paved in roof tiles. A semicircular hole, cut into one of the capstones in the south aisle (see plan, p. 39), probably marked the spot of a water feature, for the water supply to the south aisle terminated at this point. After passing beneath the *basilica*, the drain ran under the street to the north and into a yard where it emptied into a soakaway.

The rear range of rooms accommodated the offices and records of the local administration. In the centre there was the *aedes* or shrine [**4**], where statues of the emperor and civic deities would have been housed. The entrance opening on to the great hall ran the full width of the room, and the floor, at least in its later history, was raised above the floors of the rest of the *basilica*, thus giving it prominence. The room on the east side [**5**] also had a raised floor and a wide entrance, but its function is unknown. A door, marked by a threshold stone, gave access to Room **6** and from there a door,

marked by a gap in the wall, led into the larger corner room [**7**]. Both these rooms had concrete floors (now protected beneath the gravel surface) and presumably served as offices.

The largest room [**3**] served as the *curia* or council chamber. There was no direct access from the great hall into this room; its south wall survives to a height of some 6 feet (1.8m) and carried painted plaster with an architectural perspective (now removed for preservation). A row of four putlog holes, used to secure timber staging during construction, is now clearly visible. Excavation revealed that, in its later history, mosaic panels had adorned the floor (not visible) of this room, one along the west side at the entrance to the chamber, and another at right angles down the middle, thus effectively forming a T shape. Unfortunately, the mosaic had almost entirely gone and only fragments of the border were found. The rest of the room was floored with concrete. Cutting the floor on either side of the central mosaic were channels, and corresponding chases were also found in the plaster of the south wall. These carried the timber framework of the benches on which the councillors would have sat. Stone bases of a stepped wooden dais occupied the east end of the room from which the magistrates would have presided over meetings of the council. These features have not been observed anywhere else in Britain.

Rooms **1** and **2** had originally been a single chamber, and it was subdivided only at a late stage in its history. The smaller room served as a vestibule to the *curia* with benches along two walls, and the doorway from the north aisle survives beneath the modern garden wall. New side walls, built against the existing walls of the room, probably supported a stone-vaulted roof. It is possible that this strongroom may have been the civic treasury. The wall dividing the two rooms does not appear to have risen much above floor level, and it may, therefore, have carried a stone screen, with an iron grille above, behind which the cashiers worked.

The recent excavations have unravelled much of the structural history of this massive building. It was probably built in the earlier part of the second century AD, during a period that saw much municipal building in the tribal capitals of Roman Britain. The work of erecting the *forum-basilica* would have been a protracted business and must have placed a severe strain on resources and finance. The expertise required for the erection of a building of this scale and nature would have been beyond the competence of native builders at this time. Written sources reveal that elsewhere in the empire communities called on the military for assistance with civil projects. It is very likely that surveyors and architects from the Second Augustan Legion would have provided some support both in the planning and construction of the Caerwent *forum-basilica*. The excavations have also thrown much light on the various building techniques used during the construction of the building. Rare evidence for cranes and lifting devices has been uncovered, and the work has provided clear proof that the architectural embellishments, such as the columns and their Corinthian capitals, were all carved on site from local sandstone.

In the late third century, the Caerwent *basilica* appears to have been largely rebuilt. The roof of the great hall was stripped and the columns dismantled. As part of this reconstruction, certain of the walls were strengthened and the floors were also raised. These massive works may have been necessary either because of subsidence, or possibly owing to rotting timbers in the superstructure.

The *basilica* continued to function as the administrative centre until the AD 340s, but at that time the nature of its use altered. Some of the floors in the great hall were removed, and the nave was occupied by a large number of hearths, which were used by metalsmiths, perhaps for the production of nails. During this episode, which might have been quite short lived, the roof of the great hall appears to have remained intact. Some twenty or thirty years elapsed before the *basilica* was systematically demolished and the site levelled. Coins, including issues struck in the AD 390s, indicate continued frequentation of the site at this very late date. It is possible that some of the rooms surrounding the *forum* and in the rear range of the *basilica* were still in use, although the precise nature of this late occupation, at a time when the rest of the town was sliding into decay and ruin, is uncertain.

From the *forum-basilica*, you can follow the grassed footpath signposted to the Romano-Celtic temple [Panel 9]. Alternatively you can detour to view the interior of the north-east defences, across rough fields with livestock, using the signposted footpaths (p. 37).

*Top: This coin of the Emperor Trajan, minted AD 112–14, helped date the construction of the* forum-basilica *to the earlier part of the second century AD. The reverse of the coin (above) shows the public buildings that overlooked Trajan's new harbour at Ostia in Italy (National Museum of Wales).*

*A view of the council chamber, or curia, during excavation. Note the painted plaster on the standing wall at the rear, and the channels in the floor for the wooden benches (National Museum of Wales).*

# The Romano–Celtic Temple [Panel 9]

The temple complex lies near the centre of the town, to the east of the *forum*, and was excavated first in 1908 and more recently between 1984 and 1991 (see Panel 9). Built about AD 330, its plan is of a form developed by Celtic peoples of the Roman empire. Unfortunately, the excavations have thrown no light on the deity worshipped in the temple.

The temple has a square inner shrine (*cella*) with a sanctuary alcove — an unusual feature — at the back projecting into the surrounding enclosed ambulatory. The *cella*, housing the statues and cult objects, would have been raised as a tower-like structure above the lean-to roof of the ambulatory (see reconstruction drawing, p. 46). The entrance porch was, unusually, on the south side and would have contained steps to a floor level above the surrounding ground. The height of the *podium* (raised platform) on which the temple stood is unknown, for the floor levels have disappeared and only the foundations are visible. The small projections from the walls outside the temple were probably the bases for pilasters (rectangular columns attached to the wall), while those inside may mark doorways subdividing the ambulatory into separate rooms. It is assumed that the ambulatory, with a solid outer wall, provided shelter for ritual processions and perhaps the display of votive offerings.

The temple stands in a sacred enclosure (*temenos*), surrounded by boundary walls on three sides, with the fourth side fronting the main street and closed by a long hall. Architecturally, this hall was quite elaborate and was embellished with pilasters along its length — marked either by a stone base or projecting foundations. It had a tessellated floor (not visible), which was plain except for a patterned panel directly in front of the apse. The hall had central doorways in both long walls and an entrance in the short axis (indicated by two threshold stones) opposite the apsidal east end. This apse may have housed a secondary shrine. A path (now marked in gravel) led from the entrance hall to the temple proper. Few people would have been allowed into the *cella*, and most of the congregation

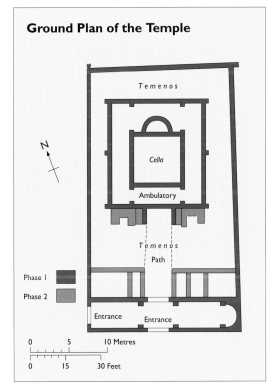

**Ground Plan of the Temple**

*Temenos*

*Cella*

Ambulatory

*Temenos*
Path

Phase 1
Phase 2

Entrance          Entrance

0     5     10 Metres
0     15     30 Feet

*Opposite: A view of the Romano-Celtic temple from the south. The temple complex was first built about AD 330.*

*A finger ring with a glass cameo in the form of an infant's head found during the excavation of the temple site (National Museum of Wales).*

would have gathered in the sacred grounds to worship and witness the ceremonies.

Later in its history, substantial alterations were made to the temple complex. A range of five rooms — now reduced largely to foundation level — was added to the inner side of the entrance hall. No specific functions could be ascribed to these rooms. At the same time, two half-domed niches — again only marked by their foundations — were built, one either side of the temple porch. They were presumably designed to hold statuary. The temple was kept in good repair until late in the fourth century.

The more recent excavations have revealed the history of the development of the plot. Before the construction of the temple, it was

*A bronze mask of Medusa from the temple site. This small boss may have decorated a wooden box (National Museum of Wales).*

*A reconstruction of the Romano-Celtic temple seen from the south-west as it may have appeared soon after construction in AD 330. The congregation would have worshipped outside in the sacred grounds (Illustration by John Banbury, 1992).*

largely occupied by an open yard, which probably formed part of the premises of a workshop to the east. The builders of the temple complex did not respect the original street lines, for both the main (east–west) and side (north–south) streets were encroached upon considerably. Belonging to the earliest phase was a large timber building of late first- or early second-century date. It comprised comfortable living quarters at the north end and a workshop with several hearths to the south. Nothing of these earlier phases is now visible.

> Return to the main street, using the accessible gate, and continue towards the car park. You may wish to visit the church, which contains the Paulinus stone and other Roman objects (see p. 31). Halfway between the church and the site of the west gate (see map, p. 31), to the north of the main street, are the remains of two Roman buildings. Turn right into Pound Lane, which is smooth and level tarmac, and you will find the site on the right side of the road [Panels 10 and 11].

*Opposite: An aerial view of the excavated shops beside Pound Lane.*

# Shops and Houses

Excavated in 1946–47, the buildings displayed in Pound Lane occupied part of the *insula* immediately to the west of the *forum* and are numbered VII.26N and 27N on the plan (inside back cover). These buildings differed in purpose and development. Building VII.26N, fronting the main Roman street, housed commercial activities as well as residential quarters. It also underwent several phases of rebuilding and alteration during its long history. In contrast, the building to the rear (VII.27N) was a courtyard house and was exclusively residential. In this case the remains belong to one period without any significant alterations.

The visible stone remains were not the first buildings on this plot. Earlier occupation in the form of a pottery kiln and a timber structure was found during excavation, mainly beneath building VII.26N. This activity dates from the later first century AD when a settlement was just beginning to develop, but there is nothing of this to see today.

# The Shops (VII.26N) [Panel 10]

The visible remains of building VII.26N [Panel 10], occupying the southern half of the site, represent several phases of construction. From the middle of the second century, the plot was occupied by two narrow strip buildings separated by a passage (now marked by the strip of grass running north–south). Both had a shop and large workroom at the front, with four or five rooms at the rear that served as the living quarters. These buildings were of single storey construction, but it is uncertain as to whether the walls stood to their full height in stone or if they

*The workshop of the west strip building was used for much of its history by a blacksmith. This relief shows a Roman blacksmith at work with some of the tools of his trade and one of his products, a lock (Museo Nazionale d'Abruzzo, Aquila, Italy/ Bridgeman Art Library).*

carried timber framework; their roofs were of tile. The floors of some of the living rooms were of concrete, while the walls were plastered and painted.

The workshop [1] of the west strip building was used by a blacksmith, for excavation revealed a hearth and scattered lumps of iron slag. The trade conducted in the east strip building is unknown, for the workshop lay beyond the area of excavation. A doorway, giving access to the passage between the two buildings, can still be seen as a break in the wall of Room **3** of the western shop. From these low ruins it is difficult to imagine the hustle and bustle that must have been associated with this busy street full of traders, and the noise and smoke that must have come from the blacksmith's shop.

At the beginning of the third century, both shops were altered and were joined together to form one building. This would indicate that one of the occupants had become wealthy enough to take over his neighbour's premises. Before these alterations were carried out, it appears that the workroom of the west shop had caught fire and was badly damaged, for there was a thick layer of charcoal in the room and outside on the road. When it was rebuilt, the front of the shop was extended over part of the main street (marked by the more southerly

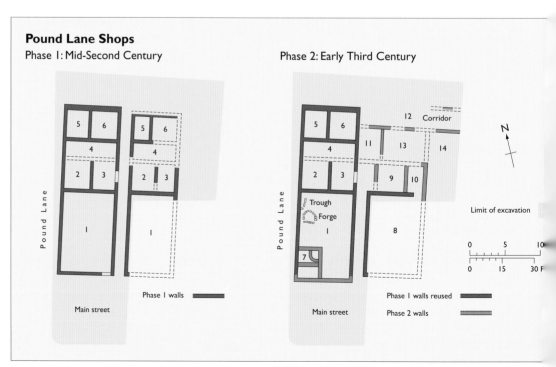

wall). The new workshop [**1**] was equipped with a forge and a rectangular quenching trough for the use of a blacksmith (these features cannot be seen today). At this time a small cubicle [**7**], possibly the shop itself, was built in the south-west corner of the workroom. It was divided into two by a cross-wall, while a quadrant-wall in one corner formed a space, which may have been used for storage. The living quarters in the west strip building [**2–6**] remained largely unchanged, but those in the east were demolished and replaced by a new series [**9–14**] opening off a corridor [**12**]. The extension of the corridor beyond the east strip building suggests the existence of additional rooms that could not be excavated.

Towards the middle of the fourth century the building was once again reorganized, and it now had the appearance of a much more prosperous property. Although the living quarters were more spacious and luxurious, the workroom of the old west strip building was still being used for commercial purposes.

A new north wing, which extended beyond the west range and impinged on the side street, replaced the earlier living rooms. The rooms tended to be larger and two [**15** and **19**] had mosaic floors (no

longer visible), indicating the increased wealth of the owners. The remains of a tiled arch between Rooms **16** and **18**, show that the owner contemplated installing a hypocaust system, but it was never constructed. In the north wall of Room **15**, there is a hole — a drain — at the level of the mosaic (now shown by gravel), enabling the floor to be swilled with water to clear away any mess possibly left from the dinner table. Another room [**17**], added slightly later, projected into the open area at the rear of the house, and it may have served as the kitchen.

Considerable alterations were carried out on the old west strip building. A new doorway, inserted in the western side of Room **2** — marked by a stone

*This tiled arch between Rooms 16 and 18 indicates that the owner considered the installation of a hypocaust system, but went no further with its construction.*

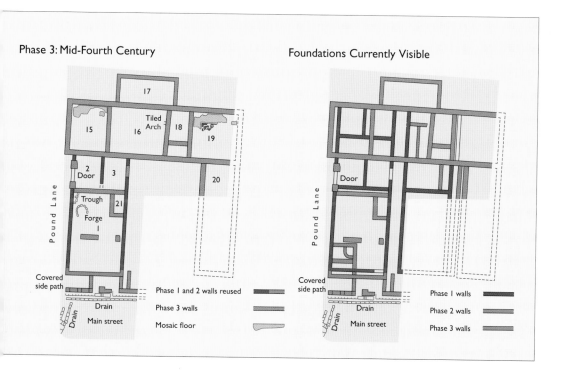

**Phase 3: Mid-Fourth Century**

**Foundations Currently Visible**

*Below: A reconstruction of a Romano-British kitchen. The cooking was done in pots and pans on a gridiron set over a charcoal fire kindled on a raised hearth. The amphorae leaning against the walls were for storage; a range of pottery, metal and glass cooking and storage vessels stand on a shelf and tables. Both of the excavated courtyard houses in the north-west corner of Caerwent may have had such well-equipped kitchens (Museum of London).*

*Below right: A painting of the mosaic pavement discovered in Room 13 of the Pound Lane courtyard house (VII.27N). The mosaic was adorned with a* cantharus *(a Greek vase) and dolphins (Illustration by David Neal).*

sill and two large sandstone blocks, which would have supported the door jambs — opened on to the side street. The old workshop [1] was subdivided by the construction of a cross-wall, but a large gap was left for access. A new north wall was also built, slightly to the south of the original one. The room was still used for commercial purposes, for the blacksmith's forge and trough were rebuilt (not displayed) at this time. In the north-east corner a small room [21] was inserted and finds on the floor included three nearly complete storage jars and the end of a lead ingot stamped (L)EG II AVG (Second Augustan Legion).

With the demolition of the old east strip building and the construction of a new wing further to the east [20], the building was now arranged round three sides of a courtyard. Before this reconstruction, the roofs had been of red tiles, but now the building was reroofed with hexagonal stone slabs, which were manufactured on site to judge from debris left behind.

The front of the house was also improved by the building of a covered footpath which encroached on the main road. The portico was paved with flagstones, and its roof was supported on columns, several bases of which can be seen. In front of this was a drain (still clearly visible), so that rainwater from the street could flow away. A further drain, originally covered with sandstone slabs, runs obliquely across the road.

The house was still occupied at the beginning of the fifth century, though in what condition is uncertain.

At this time, the occupants were using two of the former living rooms for industrial purposes (none of these features is now visible). In Room **18** two stone hearths had been laid, one of which had been built over a partially demolished dividing wall; while in Room **19**, a hearth and a pit, used in the smelting of iron, had been dug through the mosaic floor. Found among the rubbish in this room was a hoard of 150 coins, which may have been deposited only shortly before AD 425. The scattered nature of the hoard may point to its having been hidden in a loft or on a beam above, and that it became dispersed over the floor below when the house was falling into ruin.

# Courtyard House (VII.27N)

[Panel 11]

This building lies to the rear of the shops, and occupied the north-west corner of the *insula* [Panel 11]. It is part of a large courtyard house, which was constructed in the first half of the fourth century AD, doubtless by a wealthy family. Before this house was erected, the plot appears to have been open ground.

Only two wings of the house have been excavated, for the rest lies beneath an adjoining modern property. The west wing fronts on to the Roman side street, marked in part by Pound Lane. An extension to the south of the house [Rooms **6**

and **7**] restricted access from the side street into what would have been an open space (now grassed) between the two fourth-century houses.

A total of thirteen rooms of varying size is visible today. It is impossible to identify the use to which individual rooms were put, for only the lowest courses and foundations survive. However, a house of this size would have had a series of reception rooms — including a dining room — a kitchen, bedrooms and accommodation for servants.

The south wing contained five rooms [**1**–**5**], but except for Room **1**, only the southern part of the wing can now be seen. Two doorways (no longer visible) were found during excavation; one gave access to Room **2** from the courtyard, and the other connected Rooms **3** and **4**. A feature still visible is a stone plinth bedded upside down in Room **1**, which was used in a rough repair of the floor.

The west wing also had five rooms, all smaller than those in the south wing, and a passage [**11**]. No doorways were located, for the east wall had been robbed down to foundation level. Most of the rooms excavated had floors of yellow concrete. However, Room **13** (now backfilled to the top of the walls) had a mosaic pavement and was heated by a hypocaust system. The mosaic was laid on stone slabs, which were placed across the tops of sandstone pillars, beneath which the hot air circulated; the furnace was not found. There were also traces of painted wall plaster in some of the rooms showing that they had been brightly decorated. There is a possibility that part of the house had an upper storey, for it is thought that a small space [**11**] may have housed a staircase. The house was roofed with stone slabs.

The northern part of the courtyard was occupied by a walled enclosure, of which a portion can still be seen, and this is likely to have been a small garden. Part of the courtyard had been paved with flagstones, and patches are still visible.

Continue along Pound Lane northwards towards the bollards. The Roman road arrangement is shown by the gravel. The remains of a second courtyard house lie just beyond the triangular plot of ground on the left of the lane. The area in front of the courtyard house is loose gravel. The panel is across grass [Panel 12].

*Above: A total of thirteen rooms can be seen of the fourth-century courtyard house at Pound Lane (VII.27N). This view looks north-east with Room 7 in the foreground.*

**Plan of the Pound Lane Courtyard House VII.27N**

Now Covered

13

12

11

10

9

8

Pound Lane

1

2 3 4 5

6

7

Walled Enclosure

N

Limit of excavation

Culvert

0    5    10 Metres

0    15    30 Feet

*Above: This fine fourth-century mosaic was one of a number revealed during the 1981–84 excavations within the courtyard house (I.28N) in the north-west corner of the town (National Museum of Wales).*

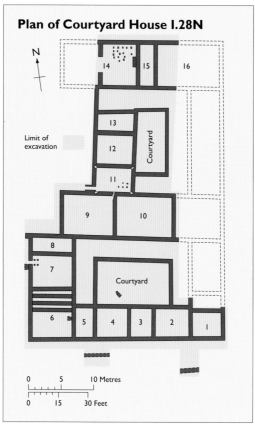

### Plan of Courtyard House I.28N

N

14   15   16

Limit of excavation

13

12

Courtyard

11

9    10

8

7

Courtyard

6    5    4    3    2    1

0        5        10 Metres

0        15        30 Feet

## Courtyard House (I.28N) [Panel 12]

This plot in the north-west corner of the town (*Insula* I) was excavated between 1981 and 1984 [Panel 12]. The lines of the roads dividing the building plots (*insulae*) are marked with gravel in the grassed area approaching the Roman remains. The earliest building (no longer visible) on this corner site was constructed in the late second or early third century AD; before that, the plot was vacant. Only a single room of this building was available for excavation. The walls, less substantial than those of the later buildings, probably stood only a few courses high, the superstructure being timber framed. A well, over 32 feet (10m) deep and probably timber lined originally, was sited immediately outside the north-west corner of the house.

In the late third century, the first building was demolished and a much larger house was constructed (no longer visible). It occupied the northern part of the plot, and the rest of the ground was enclosed for a garden and yard. The plan of this house is incomplete,

but it seems to have comprised a long central corridor, which gave access to rooms on either side. The house was one of some pretension, for there is evidence from several rooms for elaborately decorated walls and ceilings, and the central corridor had a fine mosaic.

The latest building to occupy this plot (the one which is now visible) was a very substantial dwelling providing a high standard of accommodation. Built in the early part of the fourth century, the house consisted of a number of rooms ranged around two courtyards. The courtyards are now marked by the grass areas. The walls were probably carried to their full height in stone, but only one wing of the house may have stood two storeys high, the rest being single storey. Hexagonal stone slabs, fashioned from local Old Red Sandstone, were used to roof the building. On the whole, the southern ranges were quite modest, although two of the rooms [2 and 3] had plain tessellated pavements. Another chamber was heated by a hypocaust [7] and the position of the furnace and some of the *pilae* are marked in brick. This room was very badly disturbed in the medieval period. In the south-west corner, an extremely large room [6] — with several sleeper walls to raise the floor above ground level — probably served as a store for perishable commodities, such as grain. The rooms on the northern side of the house were somewhat more elaborate and served as the main living quarters. There was much evidence for brightly painted wall plaster, and two of the principal rooms [11 and 14] were heated by hypocausts. In these rooms stone pillars (*pilae*), some of which survive, supported the raised floor under which the hot air circulated. The furnace and corner flues can still be seen in Room 11. Both of these heated rooms had patterned mosaic floors to judge from the number of tesserae found in the robbed-out basements. Room 14 is by far the largest chamber and may have served as the main dining room. The corridor surrounding three sides of the smaller northern courtyard also had a mosaic floor, with a different pattern on each side. That on the north side was made up of tesserae of blue and white lias limestone in the form of a Greek meander design, while the mosaic on the south, which was much more fragmentary, comprised a knotted or guilloche pattern. Unfortunately, the east range lies beneath the adjacent private garden, but the main entrance to the house must have been on this side, opening onto the street.

The large storeroom and the installation of a corn drier in the southern courtyard may point to this property being a farm. There were a number of small

*Left: A general view of the courtyard house (I.28N) from the south and (below) a reconstruction of the house and other buildings in* Insula I *in the fourth century (Illustration by Ian Dennis, 2005).*

buildings and walled yards in the vicinity, which may have served as barns, byres, paddocks and orchards.

The house was occupied until the second half of the fourth century, but was then abandoned and gradually fell into ruin. There are signs of extensive stone robbing in the medieval period, probably for reuse in new buildings and to feed the lime kilns.

> From here, you can return to the car park either by following the footpath northwards around the inside of the north-west defences, across a rough field with livestock, or along the signposted footpath from Pound Lane (pp. 48–51).

Recent excavations within the old farm buildings adjoining the car park suggest that the site was occupied by a combination of workshops, shops and houses opening onto the main Roman thoroughfare in a similar fashion to those on display at Pound Lane.

# Llanmelin Wood Hillfort

*Above: This early first-century AD bronze terret (rein guide) was found at Lesser Garth, Cardiff, and is representative of the magnificent metalwork found in Silurian territory (National Museum of Wales).*

Llanmelin is one of a number of medium-sized Iron Age hillforts located in Silurian territory. It is located just over a mile (2km) north-west of Caerwent, but despite its close proximity it is not thought to be the pre-Roman tribal centre of the Silures (p. 7). Indeed, there is no candidate for a tribal capital and the settlement pattern indicates a lack of political cohesion, perhaps because clan and family ties were more important than tribal ones to the Silures.

In general, defended hilltop settlements — hillforts — begin to appear from the beginning of the first millennium BC, at a time when the climate was deteriorating and new social patterns were emerging. In the Welsh borderland, the main phase of hillfort construction appears to date from the fifth and sixth centuries BC, when small (less than 6 acres, 2.5ha), univallate (single rampart) enclosures predominate. Often later enhanced with additional ramparts and more elaborate entrances, these sites could remain in use until the first century BC/AD. Whether this elaboration reflects a real or perceived threat, a form of display or the creation of enclosed space for social, economic or political activities is unclear, but the diversity of shapes and characteristics suggest a range of functions.

Llanmelin certainly seems to conform to this pattern. Surveyed by Dr R. E. M. Wheeler in 1923, the hillfort was first explored archaeologically by Dr V. E. Nash-Williams of the National Museum of Wales between 1930 and 1932, when the site was covered with woodland. More recently, topographical and geophysical surveys have been conducted by the University of Wales, Newport.

Despite the limited nature of these excavations, which consisted of a series of narrow trenches cut through the site, it seems that the hillfort began, perhaps in the third/fourth century BC or even earlier, as a simple enclosure with a single stone-revetted bank and entrances at the south and west. At the same time, a separate 'outpost' — a small earthwork enclosure — was built to the north-east of the site. Later, probably in the second century BC, the hillfort was remodelled when further banks and ditches were constructed, with a single entrance in the south-east. A third phase of building work seems to have taken place either late in the first century BC or early in the following century when the entrance was remodelled. This new in-turned entrance comprised a slightly curved passageway, probably with a wooden gate at its inner end. The banks around the entrance were faced with stone and topped with a timber platform and palisade. Probably at the same time, a series of three rectangular enclosures — the 'annexe' — was built to the south of the main camp, overlying earlier occupation deposits outside the defences. The hillfort appears to have been abandoned in the first century AD until the medieval period, when two huts were built in the ditches of the annexe.

A recent geophysical survey has revealed evidence of a number of features and has also suggested a more

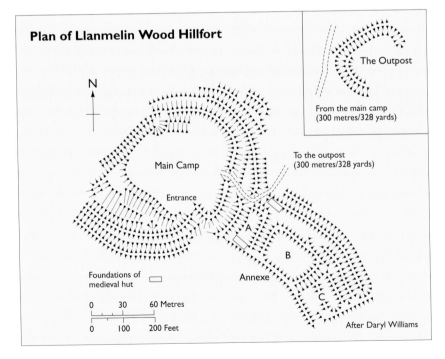

**Plan of Llanmelin Wood Hillfort**

The Outpost

From the main camp (300 metres/328 yards)

Main Camp

Entrance

To the outpost (300 metres/328 yards)

A

B

C

Annexe

Foundations of medieval hut

0   30   60 Metres
0   100   200 Feet

After Daryl Williams

complicated constructional sequence, but this requires confirmation through further excavation. It is now thought possible that one or more 'farmstead-size' enclosures may have existed on the site before the construction of the first hillfort. The survey also indicated putative roundhouses and other structures within the main enclosure of the hillfort.

## Description of the Site

Llanmelin lies on a prominent wooded spur, with steep slopes forming natural defences on all sides except the north-east. Overlooking the coastal plain of the Severn estuary, it can be approached on foot from the north of the site. The surviving earthworks comprise three distinct elements: the main camp, the annexe and the outpost.

The main camp is a multivallate enclosure, approximately 5.5 acres (2.2ha) in size. It is surrounded

*Above: An aerial view of Llanmelin Wood hillfort from the north-east. The main camp, to the right, is surrounded by two, and in places three, banks, and the in-turned entrance is on the south-east side. Geophysical survey has suggested that a number of roundhouses stood within the enclosed area. The purpose of the annexe, which was added to the main camp in the last phase of construction, is not clear, but it has been suggested that it had a funerary or ritual function (RCAHMW).*

*Left: A reconstructed Iron Age pot from Llanmelin (National Museum of Wales).*

*A late Iron Age bronze penannular brooch, with its pin now missing. It was found during V. E. Nash-Williams's excavations at Llanmelin between 1930 and 1932 (National Museum of Wales).*

by two, and in places three, large, well-preserved banks, which are highest near the in-turned entrance on the south-east side. A small stretch of what is probably part of the earliest rampart can be seen outside the main banks to the north-east.

The existing entrance to the interior is thought to be recent. Within the enclosure, various depressions mark the location of internal structures. Geophysical survey has revealed the site of numerous roundhouses — probably of timber, wattle and daub construction — some of which overlie each other indicating a complex sequence of occupation. A clay crucible with bronze adhering to the surface was found within the main camp, suggesting that metalworking took place here. Pottery fragments, animal bone from ox, horse, pig, dog and sheep (or goat), and metal objects, including parts of two bronze bracelets and a brooch, indicate occupation activity, whether seasonal, temporary or permanent.

The somewhat enigmatic annexe, roughly 2.25 acres (0.9ha) in size, was added to the south-east of the main camp during the last constructional phase of the hillfort. It consists of three rectilinear enclosures, which now have no apparent means of internal communication either between each other or with the main camp. A single external entrance exists in the south-west corner of enclosure C —

the southernmost of the three. The enclosures are seemingly devoid of Iron Age features and there was little evidence for occupation. The banks of the annexe appear to have been built over areas of charcoal containing animal bone and pottery fragments, interpreted as hearths.

Such enclosures are traditionally explained as animal corrals. However, little in the way of parallels exist for these enclosures and the discovery of two incomplete skeletons associated with the annexe — a man 25–40 years of age found in the south-west ditch of enclosure A and bones from an adult woman found scattered on the rock surface to the north-east of enclosure B — has led to the suggestion that these areas may have had a funerary or sacred rather than a domestic purpose.

The only evidence for later occupation on the site survives as the remains of two medieval huts built into the ditch of enclosure A.

The outpost consists of a semicircular earthwork and lies 275 yards (250m) to the north-east of the main camp, close to the modern road. It is now a small C-shaped enclosure, with a double embankment, but may have been circular originally. Its purpose is unknown, but it may have been associated with stock corralling; it is thought to be contemporary with the earliest phase of the main camp.

*This fragment of a clay crucible with bronze still adhering to the surface was found within the main camp at Llanmelin. It provides evidence for metalworking at the hillfort (National Museum of Wales).*

## Further Reading

### Caerwent Roman Town
M. Aldhouse-Green and R. Howell, editors, *The Gwent County History, Volume 1: Gwent in Prehistory and Early History* (Cardiff 2004).

C. J. Arnold and J. L. Davies, *Roman & Early Medieval Wales* (Stroud 2000).

T. Ashby, A. E. Hudd, F. King and A.T. Martin, 'Excavations at Caerwent, Monmouthshire, on the Site of the Romano-British City of Venta Silurum', *Archaeologia* **57–64** (1901–13).

G. C. Boon, 'The Shrine of the Head, Caerwent', in G. C. Boon and J. M. Lewis, editors, *Welsh Antiquity* (Cardiff 1976), 163–75.

G. C. Boon, 'Archaeology through the Severn Tunnel: The Caerwent Exploration Fund, 1899–1917', *Transactions of the Bristol and Gloucestershire Archaeological Society* **107** (1989), 5–26.

G. C. Boon, 'The Early Christian Church in Gwent', *Monmouthshire Antiquary* **8** (1992), 11–24.

P. J. Casey, 'Caerwent (Venta Silurum): The Excavation of the North-West Corner Tower and an Analysis of the Structural Sequence of the Defences', *Archaeologia Cambrensis* **132** (1983), 49–77.

C. Johns and T. W. Potter, *Roman Britain: Exploring the Roman World* (London 2002).

W. H. Manning, 'The Defences of Caerwent', in P. Wilson, editor, *The Archaeology of Roman Towns* (Oxford 2003), 168–83.

V. E. Nash-Williams, 'Further Excavations at Caerwent, Monmouthshire, 1923–5, *Archaeologia* **80** (1930), 229–88.

J. Wacher, *The Towns of Roman Britain*, 2nd edition (London 1995).

P. Webster, 'An Early Fort at Caerwent? A Review of the Evidence', in P. Wilson, editor, *The Archaeology of Roman Towns* (Oxford 2003), 214–20.

### Llanmelin Wood Hillfort:
V. E. Nash-Williams, 'An Early Iron Age Hill-Fort at Llanmelin, near Caerwent, Monmouthshire', *Archaeologia Cambrensis* **88** (1933), 237–346.

R. Howell and J. Pollard, 'The Iron Age: Settlement and Material Culture', in M. Aldhouse-Green and R. Howell, editors, *The Gwent County History, Volume 1: Gwent in Prehistory and Early History* (Cardiff 2004), 140–59.

D. Williams, 'Llanmelin Hillfort, Caerwent: Geophysical and Earthwork Survey' in J. Pollard et al, *Lodge Hill Camp, Caerleon, and the Hillforts of Gwent* (Forthcoming).